Music in the Classic Period

Music
in the Classic Period

An Anthology with Commentary

F. E. Kirby

SCHIRMER BOOKS
A Division of Macmillan Publishing Co., Inc.
NEW YORK

Collier Macmillan Publishers
LONDON

Schirmer Books
A Division of Macmillan Publishing Co., Inc.
866 Third Avenue, New York, N.Y. 10022

Collier Macmillan Canada, Ltd.

Library of Congress Catalog Card Number: 77–84939

Printed in the United States of America

printing number

1 2 3 4 5 6 7 8 9 10

Library of Congress Cataloging in Publication Data
Main entry under title:

Music in the classic period.

Bibliography: p.
1. Instrumental music. 2. Vocal music.
3. Classicism in music. I. Kirby, F. E.
M2.M633   780'.903'3   77-84939
ISBN 0-02-870710-9

Contents

780.9033
M98

Preface

Herewith is offered a sampling of the Western European art-music of the late eighteenth and early nineteenth centuries, representing what is commonly (rightly or wrongly) known as the Classic Period. This selection of forty compositions, most of which are given complete and in full score, endeavors to highlight the most important traditions of the age of Haydn, Mozart, and Beethoven, and of the period immediately preceding. The emphasis has been placed on instrumental music (the sonata, quartet, symphony, and concerto) and the two most important types of opera, the *opera buffa* and the German *Singspiel*. Songs and religious music, along with a great deal else, have had to be omitted.

Several factors beyond the wish to include good and representative works have influenced the selection. In the first place, an effort has been made to avoid pieces found in other readily available anthologies, such as Godwin's *Schirmer Scores* (1975), Kamien's *The Norton Scores* (1968 and various later editions), Starr and Devine's *Music Scores Omnibus*, Part I (1964; revised, 1974) and Davison and Apel's *Historical Anthology of Music*, Vol. II (1950). On the other hand, it also seemed worthwhile to include some works that are extensively discussed by Leonard G. Ratner in his *Classic Music: A Handbook for Analysis* (forthcoming). Finally, it seemed desirable to use works that are currently available in recorded form. This last criterion is somewhat problematic, but it has been met, with only one or two exceptions (most notably the fourth score, the Symphony in D by Stamitz). Yet in many cases the selections made can only be called arbitrary. Following the example of Davison and Apel, and also of Godwin, some commentary has been provided for each selection, and each chapter has an introduction. There is also a short bibliography. Thus the book is to an extent self-contained.

Given the editorial principles outlined above, it has been impossible to give in this anthology an adequate presentation of the extraordinary variety of music in the eighteenth century, especially in the time preceding Haydn, Mozart and Beethoven. The lack of suitable editions of good and representative compositions that were also available in recorded form proved too great an obstacle to overcome. In time a supplementary volume may correct this deficiency.

Permission to reproduce material under copyright has been granted by Belwin-Mills Publishing Corporation, Harvard University Press, C. F. Peters (Eulenburg Miniature Scores) and G. Schirmer, Inc. Some material from the present writer's *An Introduction to Western Music: Bach, Beethoven, Wagner, Stravinsky* (New York: The Free Press, 1970) has been incorporated into the Introduction to Chapter I and into the commentaries to Nos. 26, 28, and 29; material from his *A Short History of Keyboard Music* (New York: The Free Press, 1966) into the commentary to No. 3.

Thanks go to Arthur Miller, Librarian of Lake Forest College, and to my colleague Professor Ann Bowen, of the Music Department, for helping in a number of ways, but most especially for allowing materials in the College's collections to be used in the production of this anthology. Thanks also go to the Library of the School of Music at Northwestern University, and its librarian Don R. Roberts, where much of the work leading to the book was done. Finally, thanks go to the staff at Schirmer Books, Ken Stuart and Abbie Meyer, for work well done.

Lake Forest College   F. E. K.
July, 1977

Music in the Classic Period

1

THE BACKGROUND

THE MIDDLE OF THE EIGHTEENTH CENTURY witnessed perhaps the most comprehensive change that has ever taken place in the history of Western music.
The change in music was a natural part of the change that took place in
Western civilization generally, a change that may briefly be characterized as
involving the rise of the middle class, the bourgeoisie, to political power and
the concomitant decline of the aristocracy—in short, the formation of political
and social life as we know it today. This change in the political, economic,
and social order had a profound effect on all musical life. At bottom, it
affected the economic support for the musician. Heretofore he had been
under the patronage system, in the employment of and subservient to the
wishes of a church or court, of a bishop, an archbishop, a rector, a prince, a
duke, and so forth. But once the change had taken place, his support derived
rather from the large and generally anonymous mass audience before which
he performed his works in public concerts, and which purchased the compositions he published. The wishes and tastes of this large audience had to
be satisfied, and although the great composers' refusal to compromise brought
about an improvement in its taste, the vast majority of composers—most of
them long forgotten—contented themselves with providing works that would
gratify the mass taste and little more.

An important aspect of the socio-political-economic change in the position
of the musician and composer was a new musical style which, although affect-
ing all kinds of music, was mostly involved with instrumental music. This new
kind of music may generically be termed *galant*.[1] Its main features were
basically a homophonic texture, simple harmonies, and regularly organized,
well-balanced, easily grasped melodic phrases, the whole being unassuming,
simple, pleasing, ingratiating, and sweet. The style as a whole was derived
from the popular and unpretentious comic operas of the early and middle
eighteenth century, especially those of the so-called Neapolitan School.

In consequence of the new taste that developed in the first half of the
eighteenth century, there developed a new type of opera, the *opera buffa,* or
comic opera. The earliest of these were simple works, the two acts of which
were sandwiched in between the three acts of an *opera seria.* Unlike the
opera seria, the characters in an *opera buffa* were drawn from the contemporary middle class (not from classical antiquity, early history, or the Bible)
and frequently represented stock character-types from the popular theater, or
commedia dell'arte, of the time: the jealous and miserly old man, the shrewd
and pert servant girl, the brave young lover, the comic doctor, and so on. The
opera buffa grew into an independent genre of opera, and indeed soon
usurped the position in the repertory formerly occupied by the *opera seria.*

Yet it was instrumental music that ultimately gained the greatest importance, in contrast to the Baroque and preceding epochs. The bulk of this in-

[1] As used here, the term embraces a number of different kinds of music, from French
harpsichord music, through certain Italian operatic and instrumental compositions, to
"expressive" works by German composers of the late eighteenth century.

strumental music corresponded to the unassuming norms of the *galant*. Characteristic is the name given to many of these instrumental works—*divertimento*. Other names meaning the same thing are *cassation, nocturne,* and *serenade*. Works of this type are intended as social compositions, background music, as we would say, to social gatherings of the time.

This *galant* music was regarded as corresponding to the leading aesthetic principles of the time, which were wholly rationalistic and called for the artwork to be logically and rationally organized, clear and comprehensible to the senses. Descartes' demand for "clear and distinct" thoughts became an aesthetic requirement for the creative artist, a demand echoed by many musical theorists of the eighteenth century. At the same time, however, there ran an important countercurrent, which opposed the dominance of reason by asserting the value of imagination in an art-work. This movement came especially from England, from the writings of Anthony Ashley Cooper, third earl of Shaftesbury (1671–1713), and Edward Young (1683–1765) which became known on the Continent and there exerted considerable influence, particularly in Germany. Once the works of Shakespeare in their original versions became known, they provided a strong argument against the rationalistic conception of the artwork; and again this influence was pronounced in Germany. Finally, the poems of the alleged Celtic bard Ossian—even after the deception of James Macpherson became known—had a powerful impact.

Along with this stress on the role of the imagination in an art-work went a new interpretation of the role of the artist. This came about by virtue of the idealistic philosophy of the eighteenth century, the revival of conceptions that go back to Plato. Ultimate reality was seen to lie not in the physical world, which one perceives through the senses, but in a supersensible or metaphysical realm of ideas that lies above and beyond. The objects in the physical world were regarded as poor copies of their archetypes in the supersensible realm of ideas. In this scheme the work of art had traditionally enjoyed a peculiar position: Although it necessarily belonged to the physical world, it was also held to represent or symbolize the eternal realm of ideas. The artist thus became a sort of mediator between the supersensible realm and that of ordinary physical reality, and hence, as someone in contact somehow with this higher realm, became very special indeed. Although this idea was not new in the eighteenth century, it there took on particular importance, for in connection with the new emphasis given the role of imagination in the art-work it had a profound effect on the idea of the artist as a creator. In Shaftesbury's phrase, the artist is a "second maker, a just Prometheus, under Jove," whose creative power is seen as analogous to that of God himself. This idea represents the beginning of the "genius theory" that became so popular in the following century; and in the understanding of the eighteenth century the only genius was the artistic genius. As exponents of this idea in one way or another in the eighteenth century, we can refer to the dramatists connected with the *Sturm und Drang* movement in Germany, as well as the Weimar classical writers

Goethe, Schiller, and Herder, or, in France, Rousseau. Toward the end of the century the German philosopher Immanuel Kant set the limits to what reason can hope to accomplish, establishing the basis for the aesthetics of the nineteenth century.

This new orientation in aesthetics had its effect on music. The musical art-work, just as in the other arts, became a vehicle for expression, no longer being seen as the concrete and generalized affections of the Baroque, but rather as personal and subjective, the feelings of the artist himself. The musical art-work became the unique and individual expression of the composer. The old idea of the unity of affection prevailing throughout a composition gave way to a manifoldness, a variety of expression within a piece which usually appears as the use of more than one musical theme, frequently of themes that contrast strongly with one another. Dynamic variations, with crescendos and decrescendos, became important elements in the new music, and it is this that explains the rise of the piano in the latter half of the eighteenth century. Contrast and variety became the hallmarks of the new music.

The new expressive ideal and seriousness of purpose affected the easy, pleasant, and popular *galant* music of the time, which had to be adapted so that it could become a suitable vehicle for the new intent. This can be seen most particularly in instrumental music, which lay at the heart of the new styles. The change was primarily made by German (or German-speaking) composers who had settled in Vienna: the Hungarian Joseph Haydn (1732–1809) and the Austrian Wolfgang Amadeus Mozart (1756–1791). It is they who established the new kind of instrumental music in a way that was to remain dominant for the whole of the nineteenth century and to some extent the twentieth. Thus, they paved the way for the work of Ludwig van Beethoven (1770–1827). For this reason they, along with Beethoven, have come to be known as the Viennese Classical group of composers.

In this chapter we include works that represent what appear to be the most important types and traditions in the extremely varied time between the Baroque and the Classic. This period—in which an enormous amount of music was composed, much of it then, as now, available only in manuscript—is currently subject to a considerable amount of research, with much of the music now being published for the first time. Thus our view of this period will doubtless change considerably in the years to come.

1. Pergolesi: Two Arias from *La serva padrona* ["The Servant Mistress"]: "Sempre in contrasti"; "A Serpina penserete"

Easily the most famous among the earliest *opere buffe* is *La serva padrona* by Giovanni Battista Pergolesi (1710–1736), with libretto by L. A. Federico. It was first performed in Naples on 28 August 1733 and became known over much of Western Europe by the middle of the century, especially in Paris. Originally it was performed between the three acts of Pergolesi's serious opera *Il prigioniero superbo*. The simple plot involves the successful efforts of Serpina, the charming and scheming servant girl, to tease and torment her aging and cantankerous employer, Dr. Uberto, so that he will ultimately marry her, the main ploy being the invention of a fictitious rival, a Bulgarian captain, which eventually brings Uberto around.

The arias reproduced here represent two aspects of this work and of the genre as a whole. The first, "Sempre in contrasti" (the second in the actual work) is a typical *buffo* aria for Uberto (bass), in which he complains how he is being tormented by Serpina. Many of the devices here later became standard: the short repetitive phrases, frequently triadic and with other wide leaps but which also make much use of repeated notes (the *parlante* style), the simple accompaniment featuring tremolo and light figures, the prevailingly diatonic harmonies, and the effective use of *piano* and *forte*. In the middle section (the aria being in the *Da Capo* structure) the mock seriousness is expressed by the use of the minor.

The second aria, for Serpina, "A Serpina penserete," comes once she has threatened to leave Uberto, and tells how he will miss her. Here a rondo structure is used with the *Da Capo* (first episode, bb. 10 and 66; second, b. 37). The rondo passage is associated with Serpina's descriptions, the episodes with her comments (asides) on how the ruse is working. The first of these employs a typically Neapolitan *cantilena*, with regular phrase-structure, much use of sequence and repetition as the melody unfolds, and appoggiaturas at the ends of phrases, all with a simple accompaniment—a good instance of the *dolcezza* ("sweetness") associated with the Neapolitan style. The contrasting sections (bb. 10 ff. and 37ff.) are dance-like and comic.

Aria (*Dr. Uberto*), "Sempre in contrasti"

Uberto

that, like dog and cat, and nev-er end-ing. Where are we at? Where are we at? Now
giù; e qua e là; or ques-to ba-sti: fi-nir si può, fi-nir si può, e
=de

Uberto

this now that like dog and cat, now this now that like dog and cat, now this now
sì e no, e no e sì, e quà e là, e su e giù, e sì e

p crescendo .... a ....

Uberto

that, like dog and cat, now this now that and nev-er, nev - - - - er,
no, e no e sì, e sì e no; or que-sto ba - - - sti, ba -

.... poco .... a .... poco .... f

Uberto

- er end - ing. Now don't pre - tend your ways to end, this is the
- sti, ba - sti; fi - nir si può, fi - nir si può, fi - nir si

D. C.(¿) sino al Fine

Aria (*Serpina*), "A Serpina penserete"

11

time she was to me, she was to me. (He now
po el - la mi fu, el - la mi fu. (Ei mi

seems to be un - stead - y, not quite read - y, that I
par che già pian pia - no s'in - co - min-cia a in - te - ne -

see,... not quite read - y, no, but un - stead - y though so more
. rir,... s'in - co - min - cia, sì, già pian pia - no, sì, s'in-co -

tend - er I will be.)
. min - cia a in - te - ne - . rir.)

Sorpina

I will be, not quite read-y, no, but un-stead-y though,
-te - ne - rir, *s'in-co - min-cia, sì,* *già pian pia-no sì,*

[45]

Sorpina

so more tend - er I will be.)
s'in-co - min - cia a in-te - ne - rir.)

[50]

mf

[55]

p

Sorpina Larghetto

If at times I did dis-please you, did dis-please you, do for-
S'io poi fui im-per - ti - nen-te,im-per - ti-nen-te *mi per-*

[60]

Larghetto

cresc.

D. C. al Fine

2. Sammartini: Symphony for Strings in D Major (J.-C. 15)[1]

Active in Milan as *maestro di capella* of Santissimo Entierro from 1728 on, and later (after 1767) for Beatrice d'Este, Giovanni Battista Sammartini (1700 or 1701–1775) achieved an immense reputation all over Europe as a composer of instrumental music. Especially important are his symphonies, about seventy in number. Here both conservative and progressive aspects may be found. On the one hand, the three-movement structure in many of them comes from the overture of the Italian *opera seria*, and in many respects the influence of Vivaldi is strong. On the other, the frequent regularity of phrase structure, the simplicity and clarity in harmonic organization and texture, and the general aura of agreeableness characteristic of the *galant* testifies to the new taste.

This Symphony in D Major, apparently composed in the early 1740's, shows this mixture clearly enough. There is the three-movement arrangement, *Fast–Slow–Fast,* with the middle movement in B minor. Everything is kept very short. The first movement, Allegro, is cast in what might be called the "parallel-binary" form, in which the second half corresponds to the first except for key structure. Three distinct passages may be distinguished: first, the principal theme—eight bars long, in two parallel phrases, triadic, in octaves and unison, moving from tonic to dominant and back; the second (bb. 8 ff.)—in which the real modulation to the dominant takes place, first quasi-imitative and then figurative; third, the passage in the secondary key (bb. 20 ff.)—also in octaves and unison, with a figure in dotted rhythm. While the use of figuration suggests Vivaldi, the clear separation of contrasting elements and the general brevity are hallmarks of the new age.

The slow movement, Largo, is a short, expressive, imitative piece characterized particularly by the affective rising sixth and descending major seventh, in which all parts move exclusively in quarter-notes throughout.

[1] "J.-C." refers to the thematic catalogue of Sammartini's works compiled by Newell Jenkins and Bathia Churgin. This symphony has been recorded by Newell Jenkins with the Angelicum Orchestra of Milan on Nonesuch H 71162 and by the Camden Chamber Orchestra under John Lubbock on Oryx 1705.

The finale, Presto, shows the rounded-binary structure, with the passage between the double bar and the restatement of the opening in A minor. Light and dance-like and featuring the juxtaposition of duple and triple subdivisions of the beat, its consistency in maintaining the basic rhythmic pattern, and the resultant uniformity in character, clearly point to the Baroque. In this respect the movement compares with some of the dance movements in, for instance, Handel's concerti grossi. At the same time, its brevity, regularity of phrase-structure, and harmonic and textural simplicity suggest the new style.

Symphony for Strings in D Major

I

18

II

III

3. D. Scarlatti: Two Sonatas for Keyboard, in D Major and D Minor (K. 119, 120)[1]

A different aspect of the *galant* style may be seen in the 555 keyboard sonatas of Domenico Scarlatti (1685–1757), son of Alessandro, the famous composer of serious operas. These sonatas, composed during his long career at the Spanish court are one-movement compositions (a few of his early works are sonatas in several movements), and almost all have the same over-all formal plan: they are in binary form, or *forma bipartita*, with the double bar near the middle, each part to be repeated. It was within this simple but fundamental plan that Scarlatti was able to produce seemingly endless variety. Of some significance is the generally neglected fact that 388 of Scarlatti's sonatas are grouped in pairs, each pair being in the same tonality, and twelve more appear in groups of three sonatas, also each in the same tonality.

What makes these pieces attractive is the idiomatic treatment of the harp-sichord: the use of brilliant figuration, wide leaps, crossing of the hands, rapid reiteration of a single note, glissandi, abrupt changes of register and of texture and dynamic level, dissonance, imitation of other instruments (guitars, trumpets, etc.), his use of dance rhythms, and so on.

Scarlatti himself described them well in his preface to the set of six pub-lished in 1738: "Do not expect any profound learning, but rather an in-genious jesting with art, to accommodate you to the mastery of the harpsi-chord." Here we see something characteristic of the new *galant* taste—the emphasis on entertainment and diversion coupled with a didactic aim—so that in Scarlatti the sonata becomes, in its earliest appearance at least, associated with the etude, or teaching piece (*Handstück* in the German parlance of the later eighteenth century). But more striking is the "ingenious jesting with art," an aim that results in all the capricious elements that have been under dis-

---

[1] The "K" numbers here refer to Ralph Kirkpatrick's chronological listing of Scarlatti's sonatas. In the older listing of Alessandro Longo the numbers of these two sonatas are L. 415 and 215 respectively. Kirkpatrick's recorded performance was issued on Columbia SL–221 and reissued as Odyssey 32260007 (side 3, band 3).

cussion—"the original and happy freaks," as Burney called them, that come about from the unusual themes, harmonies, and textures, all bound up with his experimentation with the harpsichord itself and its possibilities for coloristic effects. The combination makes Scarlatti's sonatas unique not only with respect to the eighteenth century, but for the general repertory of keyboard music as well.

The pair of sonatas selected here are among Scarlatti's most capricious and brilliant. Composed apparently in the late 1740's, they belong to what Kirkpatrick refers to as Scarlatti's "flamboyant period." Structurally they fall under Kirkpatrick's "open form": the last half of each part more or less corresponds to the first, but the material immediately following the double bar has not been presented before. In the Sonata in D minor other material from the first part is restated in the second, but in a different order and with variations. Both sonatas abound in rapid figuration and wide-leaping themes, often with hand-crossings, trills, imaginative exploitation of range and texture, and unusually dissonant harmonies. Especially noteworthy in connection with this last are the *acciaccature* [2] in the Sonata in D major, as in bb. 54 ff. and 143 ff., among the more extravagant examples of this phenomenon. The principal theme of this piece, moreover, has the distinct air of a trumpet call. Such are the "original and happy freaks" of Scarlatti's sonatas.

[2] An *acciaccatura* is a dissonant ornament in which the appoggiatura is played simultaneously with the main note.

Sonata in D Major

From *60 Sonatas*, Volume One, Edited by Ralph Kirkpatrick, Copyright © 1953 by G. Schirmer, Inc. Used by permission.

Sonata in D Minor

From *60 Sonatas,* Volume One, Edited by Ralph Kirkpatrick, Copyright © 1953 by G. Schirmer, Inc. Used by permission.

4. Stamitz: Symphony in D Major
(*La melodia germanica*/op. 11 i)[1]

The Italian opera in general, and the *buffa* form in particular, found great acceptance in the rest of Europe, with the lighter comic style as we have seen it in Pergolesi and the Neapolitans gradually asserting itself over all else. Italian musicians, composers, singers and instrumentalists travelled all over Europe displaying their music and musicianship, and some of them settled down in foreign countries. This was especially true in the German cities, where the warmly-received Italian music and musicians had an enormous impact on native-born musicians.

An important center of both opera and instrumental music was the court at Mannheim under the aegis of Duke Karl Theodore, who was there from 1746 to 1778. There, in association with the performance of Italian operas, an orchestra developed that came to be famous over the entire continent. The principal artistic figure in this rise of the Mannheim orchestra was the Czech violinist, conductor, and composer Johann Stamitz (1717–1757), who came to Mannheim around 1741.

What set the tone of this Mannheim music was, in the first place, the establishment of new standards of accuracy and precision in orchestral execution; but second, and perhaps more important, was the great exploitation by Stamitz of a number of devices from the Italian music of the time. Paramount here, was the use of striking changes in dynamic level, notably the crescendo. This was usually of either the so-called "roller" type (*crescendo animé*), where a short phrase is restated several times, each statement being louder than its predecessor (later used by Beethoven and Rossini), or the "rocket" type, in which a rising triadic theme is used for the crescendo. Coupled with this was a wealth of variety and contrast in all aspects: themes, range, tempo, figuration, and so forth. Stamitz' symphonies enjoyed great popularity, so much so, in fact, that he has come to be generally regarded as the inventor of many of the

[1] This symphony has been recorded by the Munich Chamber Orchestra under Carl Gorvin (Deutsche Grammaphon Gesellschaft Archive-Produktion 3092).

35

devices found in them. Actually, his symphonies in most respects are typical of the light and engaging *sinfonia* of the Italian *opera buffa* of the time, with perhaps a little more exploitation of crescendo.

The Symphony in D Major presented here, published around the middle of the eighteenth century by Bayard (Paris) as op. 11 i, displays many of these features. It uses the three-movement structure characteristic of an Italian overture (*Fast–Slow–Fast*). In the first movement, using the sonata structure without double bar and with compression of the principal theme in the recapitulation (bb. 82 ff.), we find many themes and figures typical of the operatic overture (*sinfonia*): the regular two-plus-two–bar phrase-structure in the principal theme; much alternation between *forte* and *piano;* and the *galant* nature of the two secondary themes (bb. 24 ff. and 38 ff. in the woodwinds), the first of which is used in the development; and then there are the crescendos for which Stamitz has become famous. One should notice that the disposition of the orchestra is standard for the time: oboes and horns in pairs, and the usual complement of strings.

The second movement, an agreeable Andante in A major for strings alone, is cast in the parallel-binary form (*i.e.,* the second part is essentially a restatement of the first, but with a different sequence of keys). The short Minuet, by contrast, makes use of the full orchestra; in the Trio, also in D major, the oboes and horns are featured.

As a finale there is a Prestissimo in the sonata form. By comparison with the first movement this is shorter and generally simpler, with fewer thematic elements and great regularity in its phrase-structure. Yet the use of crescendo remains prominent, as in bb. 59 ff. As a guide to the structure, note: secondary theme, bb. 45 ff.–development, bb. 97 ff.–abbreviated recapitulation, bb. 137 ff.

Symphony in D Major

NB. Die kleinen Noten geben Varianten des Pariser Drucks.

Andante non Adagio.

Violino I.

Violino II.

Viola.

Basso.

MINUETTO.

2 Corni in D.

2 Oboi
(e Clarinetti
al unisono).

Violino I.

Violino II.

Viola.

Basso.

Fine.

5. C. P. E. Bach: Sonata for Keyboard in G Major (Wq. 55 vi)[1]

Carl Philipp Emanuel Bach (1714–1788), the oldest son of J. S. Bach, spent his career in the North, in Berlin (1740–1767) and Hamburg (1767–1788), and remained aloof from the Italian *opera buffa* and the *galant*. Famous as a composer, he also wrote an influential and comprehensive introduction to keyboard playing, the *Versuch über das wahre Art das Klavier zu spielen* (two volumes, 1753 and 1762).[2] His compositions were prevailingly serious and progressive, stressing the new genres—notably the modern sonata—and the forms and techniques that went with them. This is evident from his earliest published sonatas, the so-called "Prussian" set of 1742 (Wq. 48), and is maintained throughout his career.

A good example is a Sonata in G major from the set *für Kenner und Liebhaber* ("for connoisseurs and lovers of music"), published in 1779.[3] There are three movements in the standard *Fast—Slow—Fast* sequence, the outer movements being in the main key and cast in the sonata structure, the middle movement in G minor and in fantasia style. In the sonata structure one notes not only the variety in thematic elements (frequently almost capricious in nature) whereby small motives become important, but also the continuity in the way they succeed one another, such that each seems the inevitable consequence of what went before. In each case the development (immediately after the double bar) is based on themes introduced in the exposition. The recapitulations are at bb. 45 and 83 respectively.

The slow movement, Andante, exhibits a type of style for which C. P. E. Bach was most celebrated, *Empfindsamkeit* or "sensitivity of expression."

[1] The "Wq." numbers refer to the standard thematic catalogue of C. P. E. Bach prepared by Alfred Wotquenne.

[2] There is an English translation available by William J. Mitchell, *Essay on the True Art of Playing Keyboard Instruments* (New York, 1949).

[3] A recorded performance of this sonata, played on piano by Arthur Balsam, is on Musical Heritage Society 558.

Thematically the movement consists of figuration, scales, and broken chords, with turns, suspensions, and appoggiaturas, all played expressively and with great flexibility of rhythm, tempo and, to an extent, dynamics (see b. 12). This is particularly true of the opening bar, a long, slow line that is *senza misura* (unmeasured, to be played in free rhythm). There is no repetitive formal scheme in this movement. Rather, the piece is a continuous unfolding, leading to the deceptive cadence in E-flat major (bb. 28–9). All this was associated at the time with the fantasia, a genre prominent in C. P. E. Bach's work and that of his successors. The importance of serious expression here had a profound impact on them as well.[4]

[4] For the third of his "Württemberg Sonatas," see Joscelyn Godwin, *Schirmer Scores* (New York, 1975), No. 57, pp. 745–51.

Sonata for Keyboard in G Major

Andante.

Allegro di molto.

6. Gluck: Excerpt (Act I, Scenes 1 and 2) from *Orfeo ed Euridice*

An important episode in the music of the late eighteenth century was the so-called reform of the *opera seria* undertaken in Vienna in the 1760s by the composer Christoph Willibald Gluck (1714–1787) and the librettist Raniero di Calsabigi (1714–1795) under the sponsorship of Count Jacob Durazzo, superintendent of the Imperial Court Theater. The three relevant works here were *Orfeo ed Euridice* (1762), *Alceste* (1767), and *Paride ed Elena* (1770); later Gluck produced a series of operas in Paris, two of which are revisions of the Vienna works.

This reform [1] represents a reaction against the old established form of *opera seria* as represented by the libretti of the great Italian poet Pietro Metastasio. These featured, along with complex plots and an emphasis on the spectacular, numerous long arias intended more to provide singers (foremost among whom were the castrati) with opportunities for bravura display than to work meaningfully with the drama. Essentially Gluck and Calsabigi reshaped this, in part under the influence of the French *tragèdie lyrique,* by placing dramatic values first: thus, the actions became simplified so that there was but one main line in the plot, recitative increased in significance (the *secco* [2] type was eliminated altogether), the arias became shorter, virtuoso elements were cut down if not virtually eliminated—in short, everything became simple and direct. Two elements largely foreign to the Italian opera but important in the French were given prominence: the chorus and the ballet. The whole enterprise may be characterized by the famous phrase of Winckelmann, the noted art historian of the time: "noble simplicity and quiet grandeur."

---

[1] The tenets of their work were set forth in several letters and prefaces, among which the preface to *Alceste* and Gluck's letter to the *Mercure de France* of 1773 are important; both are readily available in Strunk's *Source Readings in Music History* (New York, 1950), Nos. 71 and 73 respectively.

[2] Recitative accompanied only by the continuo (keyboard instrument and violoncello or viola da gamba).

The old story of Orpheus is admirably suited to this notion. Indeed it figured prominently in the earliest days of opera, and on and off ever since. The Greek legend provides good ground for these ideas: the famous musician, who through the power of his song has been able to bring his wife Eurydice back from death, then fails to fulfill the one condition imposed, that he not give in to her desperate entreaties and look back upon her until they have left the underworld.

The opening scenes, reproduced here from the French version, show Gluck's and Calsabigi's principles at work. Orpheus' mourning for the dead Eurydice is represented here in two large adjacent sections, each of which is organized by a refrain structure. In the first, the refrain element is the solemn lament of the chorus, punctuated by interjections from Orpheus. In between the sections is a recitative for Orpheus and a short ballet.[3] In the second, the refrain element is Orpheus' aria, in three strophes, in between which he again sings recitatives. Particularly noteworthy are the great importance given to the chorus, the strophic structure of the aria (not characteristic of Italian opera), and the general lack of embellishment. The refrain structure, the general brevity of the elements, the use of chorus and ballet—all are more characteristic of French opera at the time.

[3] For another ballet from *Orfeo ed Euridice*, see Godwin, *Schirmer Scores*, No. 12, pp. 80–6.

Excerpt (Act I, Scenes 1 and 2) from *Orfeo ed Euridice*

An attractive, secluded grove of laurel and cypress trees surrounding a clearing on which is seen the grave of Euridice. A group of shepherds and shepherdesses are decorating the grave with flowers; others throw incense on the sacrificial flame. Orpheus, slightly downstage from the group, is leaning against a rock and occasionally joins in the lament of the chorus.

SCENE I

Orpheus. Shepherds and Shepherdesses

No. 1 Chorus

From *Orpheus and Euridice*, vocal score. Copyright © 1957, 1959 by G. Schirmer, Inc. Used by permission.

No. 2 Recitative

Orpheus *Orphée*

Your sor - row and your grief In - crease my des - o -
Vos plain - tes, vos re - grets aug - men - tent mon sup -

la - tion. In fi - nal, de - vout in - vo - ca - tion Ap -
pli - ce! Aux ma - nes' sa - cres d'Eu - ri - di - ce ren -

peal to her gods in your gloom By strewing flow-ers on her tomb!
dez les su - prê - mes hon - neurs, et couvres son tom - beau de fleurs.

No. 3 Pantomime

Lento

No. 4 Chorus

No. 5 Recitative

Orpheus ʋrphée

I bid you leave. A - lone my sor - row - strick - en
É - loi - gnez - vous; ce lieu con - vient à ma dou -

breast Shall once more sigh her name Where in death she will rest.
leur, et je veux sans té - moins y ré - pan - dre des pleurs.

No. 6 Ritornello

(The chorus exits.)-(Les bergers et les nymphes se dispersent dans le bois.)

SCENE II
Orpheus

No. 7 Aria

No. 8 Recitative

No. 9 Aria

No. 10 Recitative

Orpheus *Orphée*

Ah, be - lov - ed, my be - lov - ed! All that I see
Eu - ri - di - ce, Eu - ri - di - ce! *de ce doux nom*

sings me your name. The brook sings its praise to the trees, And the
tout re - ten - tit, *ces bois, ces rochers, ce val - lon.* *Sur les*

leaves to the stones. Cut in branch - es, the name of Eu - ri - di - ce will sing of
troncs dé - pouillés, *sur l'é - cor - ce nais - san - te on lit ce mot gra - ve* *par*

hap-pi-ness and beau-ty.
u - ne main trem-blan-te.

Eu - ri - di-ce has died, Death I myself pre-
Eu-ri - di - ce n'est plus, et je respire en-

20

fer. Gods, give her back to me ___ Or let me die with her!
cor. Dieux, ren-dez - lui la vi - e, ou don-nez-moi la mort!

Andantino   **No. 11 Aria**

Orpheus *Orphée*

Filled with ___ woe ___ and de - spair, Rend-ing ___ with ___ sighs ___ the ___
Plein de ___ trouble et d'ef - froi, que de ___ maux loin ___ de

10

air, ___ My heart is ___ sink ___ ing, ___ My heart ___ is ___ sink -
toi, ___ mon cœur en - du - ré, mon cœur en - du -

I

ing.   The brook a - lone ___ shall know ___ How
ré;   té - moins de ___ mes ___ mal - heurs, ___ sen -

2

HAYDN

FRANZ JOSEF HAYDN (1732–1809) is generally regarded as responsible for the establishment of the aesthetics, styles, techniques, and structural principles of the new art of instrumental music in a form that made them "classic" in an accepted sense of the term: worthy of being imitated and held up as models for future work. Yet this process in which Haydn gathered in from the immense variety of music of the time and then made adaptations for his own use took many years. While his work embraced all genres of musical composition, it was the instrumental compositions that proved to be decisive; these are stressed in this chapter, which will attempt to illustrate his consistent development from one state to the next.

Born in rural surroundings, Haydn was brought to Vienna in 1740 to serve as choirboy at St. Stephen's Cathedral. When his voice broke in 1749 he was released, and for a decade led a hard life in the city, studying, taking odd jobs here and there, participating in and absorbing as much as possible from the musical activities. Then in 1759 he became music director to Count Morzin in Vienna and Lukavec. Two years later he was engaged by the famous Esterhazy family, with whom he remained associated for the rest of his life. As he composed and published more and more works, his fame grew, and he eventually came to be regarded as one of the foremost composers of his age. In 1791–2 and again in 1794–5, at the pinnacle of his success, he gave concerts in London featuring symphonies written specifically for these occasions.

7. String Quartet in B-flat Major (op. 1 i)

Since the string quartet occupies a position of paramount importance in Haydn's work as a composer—such that it is possible to represent in all essentials his artistic development through this genre alone—it is fitting to commence with his very first venture, and, indeed, to end with his last. Composed sometime before 1760, the Quartet in B-flat, like the other early quartets, is a modest work related to the suite or partita (also known as *quadri* or *cassatio*) —in short, is a serenade, composed in the *galant* style so popular at the time. The five-movement structure is characteristic of the Viennese serenade: The three main movements, *Fast—Slow—Fast*, are separated by two minuets with trios. In a later development, one of the minuets was dropped, producing the structure that became the norm for the string quartet, identical with the scheme of the later symphony. The first and last movements (and the second minuet, in the serenade form) are in the main key; the two others, the first minuet and the Adagio (slow movement), stand in subdominant relation to this main key. (Both trios are in the same key as the minuets with which they are associated.) This piece and its companions are not really chamber music in our sense of the term: They may well have been performed by a small orchestra, rather than by a group of soloists.

The two movements that use the sonata structure are on a small scale. In the first, Presto, the principal theme itself exhibits a dualistic structure, with two contrasting elements (each two bars long) heard twice, with small changes. The transition leads to the dominant (reached by b. 14), and after a short pause a thematic element in the secondary key (dominant) is presented (b. 17), consisting of broken, descending seventh-chords in sixteenth-note motion. A brief four-bar passage concludes the exposition. The development, very short (sixteen bars) uses this secondary theme in alternation with part of the principal theme. In the light Finale, also Presto, the sonata structure is also handled simply and concisely. Here, since the secondary theme (b. 18) uses the same figure as the principal theme, the form is monothematic; this figure also dominates the development, which is very short (bb. 28–41).

The slow movement, Adagio, the heart of the serenade, is a melodious piece where the first violin has all the thematic interest. It uses a good deal of

79

figuration and some wide leaps, while the rest of the ensemble provides an unobtrusive, constantly moving accompaniment. Thus this movement is much like a real serenade, even though the accompaniment does not suggest the mandolin or guitar. Structurally there are two main parts, almost like strophes in a song, the last sections of which are substantially the same (first part, bb. 5–18—second part, bb. 19–37; bb. 12–18 correspond to bb. 31–7). There is a short introduction and a coda.

Of the two minuets, the first is lyrical, while the second is sturdy and folksy, with some contrapuntal interest and irregularity in the phrase-structure. The trio of the first accords well in the way the ensemble is treated with the designation given Haydn's quartets of op. 2 by their French publishers: "quartets dialogués." The other trio is quite regular.

The general aura of simplicity and conventionality of this piece may be found in most of Haydn's earlier work in all genres. The popular *galant* style provided, as it were, the ground from which his later and more elaborate compositions were to grow.

String Quartet in B-flat Major

I

Reprinted from Eulenberg Pocket Scores by permission of the publisher, Ernst Eulenberg, Ltd.

II

Menuetto D.C.

III

IV

M. D. C.

V

8. Allegro di molto (Second Movement), from the Symphony in F Minor (No. 35a or 49, *La passione*)[1]

In 1766 Haydn's patron, Nicholas (known as "The Magnificent"), completed the construction of the palatial residence of the Esterhazy family, *Esterháza*, near Vienna. This building, intended to rival Versailles in splendor, was to be Haydn's home for roughly twenty-five years, and was the scene of a rich and varied cultural life. Haydn reported (to his biographer Griesinger) on the conditions there in the following terms: [2]

> My prince was pleased with all my works, I received applause, as conductor of the orchestra I could experiment, observe what made an impression and what weakened it, thus could venture to improve, make additions, make cuts. I was isolated from the world, no one near me could confuse and torment me, and so I had to become original.

This originality has naturally been much discussed. There is no doubt that a number of remarkable (and in some cases extreme) works were composed in the six years following the completion of Esterháza. Haydn's intention evidently was to go beyond the purely *galant*, as represented by the Quartet in B-flat major and many other early works, to produce compositions on a larger scale, of greater scope, with more intensity of expression—in short, serious pieces, of considerable weight and importance.

Perhaps the most radical among these is the Symphony in F minor, composed in 1768 with the appropriate title, "La passione," added by the French publisher. The key of F minor was often used for somber and supernatural scenes (the so-called *ombra* and *orrore* scenes) as well as for the expression

---

[1] The editors of the first collected edition of Haydn's symphonies thought this work had been composed around 1773, as No. 49. Subsequently it was discovered to have been composed five years earlier, just after No. 35.

[2] Translation by F. E. K.

of agitated passion, and was so understood by Beethoven. Consistency throughout the work is promoted by the use of F as the tonic in all movements. Moreover, the symphony, which is scored for a normal combination of instruments,
is cast in an old-fashioned form, the *sonata da chiesa* (church sonata): four
movements, *Slow—Fast—Slow* (here, Minuet and Trio)—*Fast*. But the main
point is the violent expression of passion, particularly in the second movement,
which is herein reproduced. One may note the principal theme with its wide
leaps accompanied by sharply articulated scale-figuration, the use of short
motives, syncopation, sudden dynamic changes, and so on.

A model for much of this was doubtless found by Haydn in the work of
C. P. E. Bach, who also went beyond the *galant* in much the same fashion.
In Bach's case this was to an extent related to the taste of Northern Germany,
which remained rather conservative and oriented to the Baroque, even until
the early nineteenth century. His seriousness of purpose and intensity of expression seem to have had great impact on Haydn in these years.

Finally, the extreme expressiveness in this work, and in others written at
the same time, has been associated with the literary movement known as
Sturm und Drang; this phase in Haydn's development has also been referred
to as a "romantic crisis" (see Geiringer).

Allegro di molto from Symphony No. 35a or 49 in F Minor
(*La passione*)

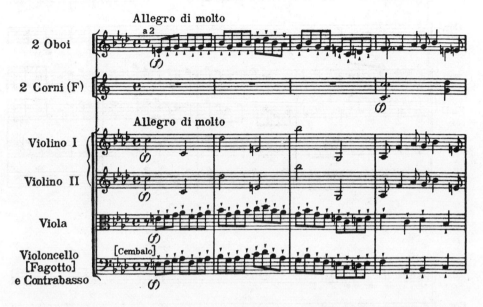

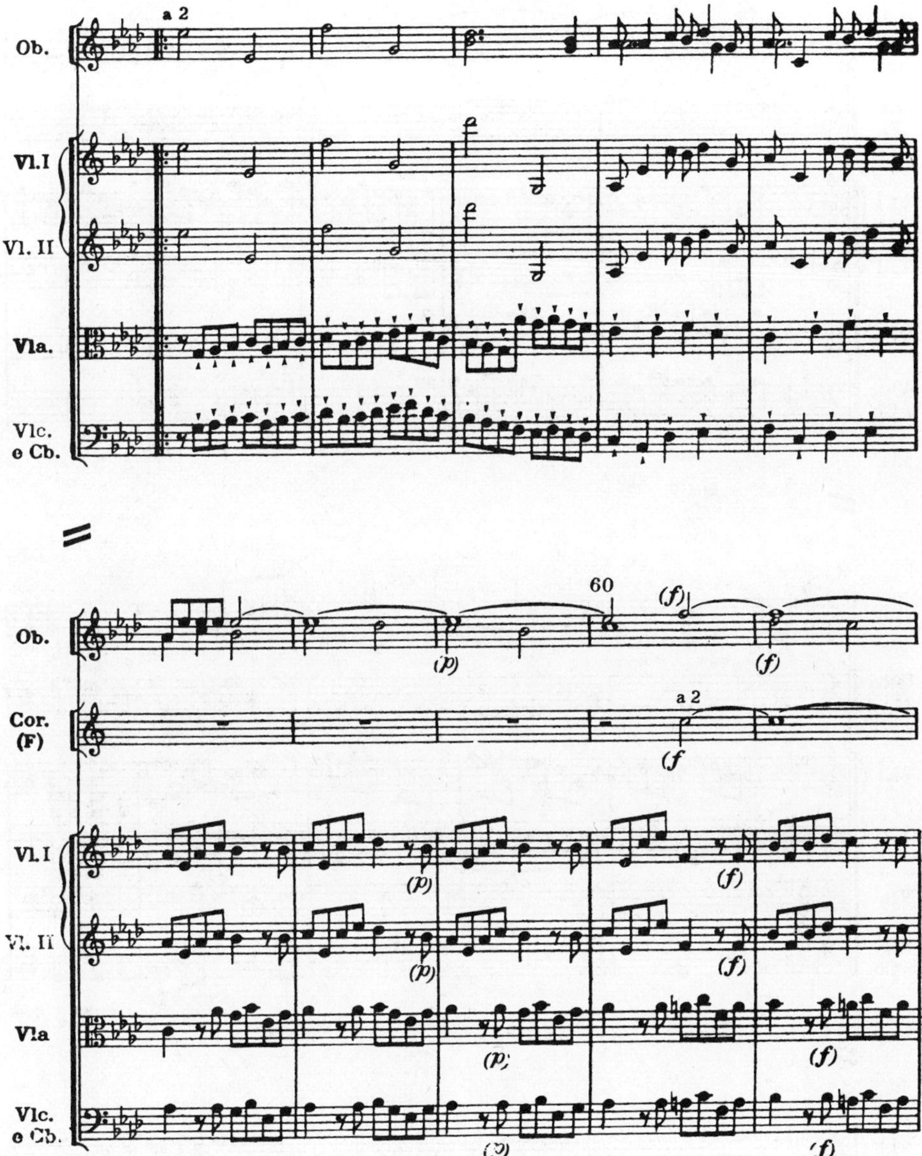
a 2
Ob.
Vl. I
Vl. II
Vla.
Vlc.
e Cb.
60
(f)
(p)
Cor.
(F)
a 2
(f
(p)
(f)

9. String Quartet in C Major (op. 20 ii)

With the six quartets of op. 20, composed in 1772, Haydn carried further the tendencies towards a more serious tone and greater expressive range that we found in the Symphony in F minor, while moderating the extreme nature of the expression in that work. In this respect a nice comparison would be between the symphony and the quartet in the same key (op. 20 v). At the same time, we note the effort to achieve even greater continuity in the four individual movements, which are now conceived as a coherent whole, coupled with greater elaborateness in part-writing, harmony, and in the use of motivic themes. The appearance of fugues in three of the finales is an external sign of this preoccupation.

The Quartet in C major provides a good illustration. All four movements are in C (the second in C minor), and the middle two are to be played with no pause between them, so that continuity is stressed and contrast minimized. Seriousness, elaborateness, and intensity of expression prevail. Much of this is evident at the outset in the continuity in phrase-structure of the principal theme, the way it is driven forward by reiteration of the small motivic particle, its contrapuntal nature, and the use of the motive later in the movement.

The slow movement, Adagio, was designated "Capriccio" in Haydn's copy, a term which at the time meant something akin to "fantasia" (see above, pp. 52–53). Here the conception is of an operatic scene, but in terms of the string quartet: passages in the styles of an accompanied recitative, an arioso, and an aria follow one another. The first four bars make up the opening tutti (the ritornello), repeated by the arioso-like violoncello solo, followed by rapid interchanges among the whole ensemble, like a passionate recitative (the expressive figurations in the first violin here, in bb. 14–16, recall C. P. E. Bach). With the aria proper, in E-flat major (bb. 34 ff.), everything becomes simpler and more conventional, yet even here the expressive element intrudes (bb. 47–52, 54, 57, 59, etc.).

Contrapuntal part-writing and chromatic harmony characterize the Minuetto and Trio. The latter, rather exceptionally, is not in the rounded-binary structure; furthermore, its second part tends to recapture the atmosphere of the beginning of the Adagio.

The finale, a fugue with four subjects (appearing in the first violin, bb. 1–3; viola, bb. 2–4; first violin, bb. 3–5; and first violin, b. 12, respectively), follows many conventions from the Baroque: the forward drive, the continuity, the use of stretto and even of inversion (which Haydn marks *al rovescio*, b. 103), and pedal points (bb. 114–19 and 146–51). None of this, of course, is characteristic of the *galant* style. Haydn here is aiming at an audience of connoisseurs who are not content with mere gratification and entertainment. Although the fugue was thought of at the time as learned, a little old-fashioned, and by no means *galant*, its use here as the finale, a culmination capping off, as it were, the whole work, provided a model followed by other leading composers, notably Mozart and Beethoven.

String Quartet in C Major

I

Reprinted from Eulenberg Pocket Scores by permission of the publisher, Ernst Eulenberg, Ltd.

II

Segue Menuetto

III

Menuetto. Allegretto

Menuetto D.C.

Fuga a IV Soggetti

IV

10. String Quartet in G Major (op. 33 v)

Haydn apparently felt that with the works he had composed in the years 1768–72 he had reached an ending point, particularly in the string quartet. For in the next ten years he abandoned this genre altogether, turning his attention to others. When he once more took up the string quartet in 1781 with the six quartets of op. 33, he described them in two letters as being "of a new and special kind," making specific reference to the ten-year hiatus in quartet composition. With these pieces Haydn is generally regarded as having formulated the mature classical style of composition.

Just exactly what this "new and special kind" refers to has been much debated. The view that here for the first time Haydn systematically employed the technique of thematic and motivic development must surely be rejected in view of what he and others, notably C. P. E. Bach, had already accomplished. Yet these pieces do mark a change in orientation from his last efforts in the genre: the sense of continuous progression, the unfolding of a single expressive character, has been abandoned in favor of balance and contrast among the four movements. Thus the old classical ideal of harmony in an art-work as a *coincidentia oppositorum* (agreement of opposites) is reestablished. In a way this is a return to the aesthetics of his earliest, *galant* quartet works; the difference, and it is important, is that none of the intensity of expression, seriousness, elaboration, and complexity (notably in the contrapuntal part-writing where all four instruments present and develop thematic material) has been given up. We thus have a revival of the old without abandoning what had been gained in the meantime.

In these quartets the four-movement scheme is established, with each one having its own expressive quality. The structural types used are also set, although there remains room for freedom here: the sonata structure for the first movement; aria-like forms for the slow movement; minuets or (as below) scherzi,[1] both with trios, for the dance movement; and for the finale usually the sonata or the sonata-rondo structure, but occasionally something

---

[1] "Scherzo" basically means fast minuet. The appearance of the scherzo here has caused all six pieces in the entire opus to be known as "the scherzi"; or, in view of the dedication to Grand Duke Paul of Russia, they are also known as "the Russian quartets."

else, such as theme-and-variations. The greatest importance is given to the sonata structure, where the themes used display great regularity and simplicity of construction, while being compounded of small thematic motives and figures which are manipulated separately and in countless combinations to generate the rest of the movement. Frequently these themes are not especially individual or striking; it is what can be done with them that counts.

The Quartet in G major (which in the original edition, published by Artaria in Vienna, appeared as the first of the six pieces in op. 33 [2]) shows most of this clearly enough. Its four movements exhibit great variety and contrast despite the fact that all, even the Trio, are in the same tonality, G major.

The first movement, Vivace assai, in sonata form, uses a principal theme consisting of three distinct elements (bb. 2, 7 and 10), though Rosen points out the wit of also placing the cadential formula at the very beginning.[3] Elements of this theme dominate almost everything that follows: the transition (b. 24), where some "developing" takes place, and the closing passage (b. 64), the exception being the secondary or "relief" theme [4] (b. 48). In the development (b. 95) all thematic elements are explored: first the principal theme, then the relief theme (b. 131), finally the closing passage (b. 152). The recapitulation is at b. 181, with the close being cut down and replaced in part by a coda (bb. 271 ff.).

The slow movement, Largo and cantabile, in G minor, is a lyrical serenade or aria in the gentle *pathétique* style for the first violin, the remaining instruments each fulfilling a set role in the accompaniment. Moreover, the aria form is also suggested by the three-part structure (middle section, b. 9; restatement, b. 30). Just as the aria is about to conclude, a long insertion in the fantasia or expressive recitative style appears (bb. 39–51), after which comes the expected ending.

In the Scherzo we meet with syncopation, something often used by Haydn in this type of movement. There is also a false recapitulation of a sort at b. 16 (in the dominant). The Trio displays two-part writing in its second section, something also frequently encountered in Haydn.

Rather unusually, the finale is a theme-and-variations on a popular type of theme, using the *gigue* rhythm with regular phrases in binary form. The variations are simple: the first (b. 16) displays ornamentation in the first violin, the second (b. 32) works with a rhythmic figure prominent in the theme, and the third (b. 48) features ornamentation alternately in the violoncello and the viola. The coda (Presto), based on a variant of the theme, starts at b. 80.

[2] The order used now appeared first in the collected edition of the quartets published by Pleyel, which apparently followed the edition published by Seiber in Paris (1783). See Charles Rosen, *The Classical Style: Haydn, Mozart, Beethoven* (reprint edition, New York, 1972), Preface to Norton Library Edition, p. xi.

[3] Rosen, *The Classical Style*, p. 78.

[4] This nice term appears to have been coined by Denis Forman in his *Mozart's Concerto Form: The First Movements of the Piano Concertos* (New York, 1971).

String Quartet in G Major

I

Reprinted from Eulenberg Pocket Scores by permission of the publisher, Ernst Eulenberg, Ltd.

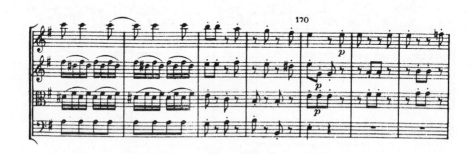

II

Largo
Cantabile

III

Trio

Scherzo D. C. al Fine

IV

Finale
Allegretto

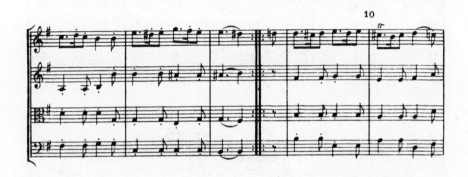

11. Symphony No. 99 in E-flat Major

Composed in Vienna late in 1793,[1] this is the first in the second series of symphonies Haydn gave in London in the 1794–95 season at the Salomon concerts. It may be regarded as representative of the fully-developed classical symphony, at once the culmination of Haydn's work in this genre and the model for much that was to follow. Scored for a normally large orchestra for the time (presumably an ensemble of around sixty musicians), the work in its four contrasting movements possesses great variety, featuring brilliant figuration and memorable touches in instrumentation. Clearly the whole is designed to entertain, in the highest sense of the word, a large public audience.

After a slow introduction (Adagio), in which the portentous gives way to expressive figuration, the sonata-form Vivace gets underway (b. 19). Noteworthy here are: the catchy principal theme with its regular phrase-structure, first stated *piano* in the strings and then *forte* by the full orchestra; the brilliant transition; the restatement of the principal theme in the dominant (b. 48); and the lyrical and "popular-sounding" relief theme (b. 71). Both figure in the development (bb. 90 ff.). The recapitulation is at b. 138, with a short developmental coda (bb. 162 ff.).

The Adagio second movement in G major (also in sonata form) has all the seriousness associated with this tempo-marking at the time. Its lyric, measured principal theme, continued fugally in the woodwinds (bb. 16 ff.), leads to the expressive secondary theme (bb. 27 ff.) near the end of the exposition. The short development (bb. 35 ff.) works with this secondary theme and includes a passage in the *Sturm-und-Drang* style (bb. 47 ff.). The recapitulation is at b. 54; the coda (b. 78) draws on the secondary theme (b. 89).

After a light Minuet with some motivic interplay and a waltz-like Trio in C major comes the brilliant finale. This presents a good but somewhat irregular example of the so-called sonata–rondo frequently encountered in Haydn. It embraces *galant*, "popular" themes, sudden loud passages with brilliant figuration, some use of counterpoint, and even a sort of joke (bb. 196–200). The

---

[1] For another of Haydn's "London" symphonies, No. 100 in G major (the "Military"), see Godwin, *Schirmer Scores*, No. 59, pp. 809–56.

157

rondo or refrain itself (not unusually in rounded–binary form, but here with everything in the second part written out) reappears later in shortened form at b. 112, but not near the end, as would be expected. The contrasting episode (b. 67) is approached with a transition passage (bb. 32 ff.; the episode's reappearance is at b. 222). Contrapuntal work based on the principal theme figures importantly in the ensuing development (bb. 132 ff.). The coda comes at b. 258.

Symphony No. 99 in E-flat Major

I

II

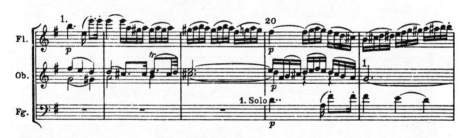

III

Menuetto. Allegretto

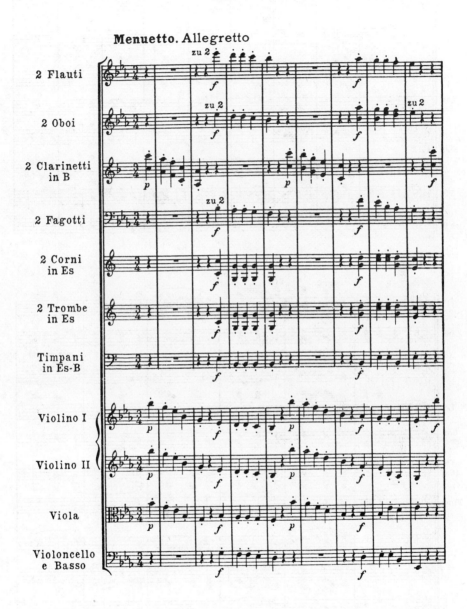

IV

270

Laus Deo

12. Sonata for Piano in E-flat Major (No. 52)

A work composed in the same place and around the same time as the Symphony No. 99 (and in the same key) is this large piano sonata. Up to the 1780s and 1790s the sonata as a genre was not ordinarily made the vehicle for large, elaborate, and intense compositions, but rather was kept smaller and more modest, suitable for diversion of the lighter kind and for teaching—in short, conforming to the ideals of the *galant*. This applies to most, but by no means all, of the sonatas by Haydn and Mozart, and even to some by Beethoven.

This work, however, is a notable exception, as is clear from its size and scope, and its resourcefulness in exploiting the range, power, and sheer sound-capacity of the new keyboard instrument. While one can make a case for it as harpsichord music, as Ratner does, it also seems well-suited to the piano. Here one can refer to the sonatas of Muzio Clementi, which Haydn doubtless knew; both make idiomatic use of the resources of the piano, particularly as manufactured by John Broadwood at the time.

The sonata is in three movements: a broad Allegro moderato in sonata form, an ornamental Adagio in E major (unusual for a work in E-flat major) and in three-part form, and a brilliant Presto, also in sonata form. We will here merely outline the structure of the three movements.

First movement. A second principal theme appears at b. 6; the modulating passage, based on the first principal theme, at b. 9; the secondary theme, also based on the first principal theme, at b. 17; the closing section of the exposition starts with the capricious tune at b. 27, with the first principal theme reappearing at b. 33. The development (b. 44 ff.) works mostly with the closing theme (note particularly the passage in E major, b. 68 ff., doubtless preparing the way for the second-movement Adagio), and features brilliant figuration. The recapitulation is at b. 79.

Second movement. This is in three-part form with the middle section at b. 19 and the restatement of the first at b. 33. The first part in its initial presentation is in rounded-binary form.

Third movement. Again there is a second principal theme (b. 16 ff.); the modulatory passage is at b. 28; the secondary theme, consisting of broken chords, is at b. 65, with a closing part at b. 78. The development (b. 102 ff.) works with most of these; the recapitulation, after a fantasia-like passage, comes at b. 203.

Sonata No. 52 for Piano in E-flat Major

Finale.
Presto.

13. Recitative and Chorus, "Die Himmel erzählen," from *Die Schöpfung* ["The Creation"]

During his first visit to London Haydn attended the first festival devoted to Handel and was profoundly impressed, particularly by the grandeur of the choral pieces in the oratorios. When he returned to the service of the Esterhazys in 1795 and was called upon to produce religious compositions for chorus and orchestra, he gave much room to large and impressive settings using chorus.

Apart from a number of masses, the influence of Handel is most clearly seen in the two oratorios *The Creation* and *The Seasons*, both of which take their texts, appropriately enough, from English sources. *The Creation* is based on the book of Genesis, parts of Milton's *Paradise Lost*, and selections from the psalms, all selected and adapted for use in an oratorio. The German translation was by Baron Gottfried van Swieten, himself a great admirer and promoter of the music of Handel and Bach. It was first performed in Vienna with great success on 29 and 30 April 1798, repeated the following year, and published the year after. With the role of *testo* (narrator) shared by three archangels, the events of the seven days of Creation are recounted by means of recitatives, arias, ensemble pieces and choruses; everything abounds in pictorial and mimetic touches, such as the famous portrayal of chaos at the outset, the celebrated and effective setting of "Let there be light," the representations of thunder, lightning, rain, animals and fish, and so on. The third part of the oratorio is devoted to the praise of creation by Adam and Eve.

The excerpt included here, the end of Part I, shows much of this. The accompanied recitative for Uriel (tenor), as part of the *testo* role, portrays first the sunrise, by means of an orchestral crescendo in which the first violins (with flutes doubling) ascend a tenth in half-notes as the bass descends, culminating in a martial fanfare in D major. Next comes the rising of the moon, a subdued passage in the strings using suspensions. Then, in conventional

244

recitative style comes the exhortation to give praise, which leads directly to the great fugal chorus, "Die Himmel erzählen die Ehre Gottes" ("The Heavens Are Telling the Glory of God"); the text is from Psalm 19.

This popular chorus clearly shows in its size and expressive power the influence of Handel. The addition of trombones to the orchestra here is significant, the use of this instrument being reserved at the time for occasions of seriousness and weight. A refrain pattern dominates the first part of the chorus, with the strong homophonic tutti of the choir alternating with episodes for the three soloists (bb. 19 ff. and 54 ff., respectively). The last of these episodes is contrapuntal, with expressive repetitions and pauses at its end (bb. 84 ff.). The last statement of the refrain (at b. 94) leads directly to a fugue on a subject derived from the refrain theme and based on the ascending hexachord; this fugue features sequential writing, and employs stretto (as in bb. 120 ff.) and inversion (bb. 123 ff.), all accompanied by continuous figuration in the orchestra. All of this is typical of a Baroque fugue, as is also the impressive pedal point on the dominant (bb. 159–66). A remarkable culminating passage commences at b. 174, the powerful bass rising by semitones and then descending by interlocking thirds. The successive harmonic points here (featuring diminished-seventh and augmented-sixth chords) are emphasized first by upbeats of two eighth-notes, then by triplets and sixteenths, leading to the final cadence where the plagal effect is pronounced.

Text and translation

RECITATIVE (No. 12)

URIEL:

In vollem Glanze steiget jetzt die Sonne strahlend auf, ein wonnevoller Bräutigam,	In splendor bright is rising now the sun, And darts his rays; a joyful, happy spouse,
ein Riese, stolz und froh, zu rennen seine Bahn. Mit leisem Gang und sanftem Schimmer schleicht der Mond die stille Nacht hindurch. Den ausgedehnten Himmelsraum ziert ohne Zahl der hellen Sterne Gold.	A giant proud and glad To run his measur'd course. With softer beams, and milder light, Steps on the silver moon through silent night; The space immense of th' azure sky A countless host of radiant orbs adorns.
Und die Söhne Gottes verkündigten den vierten Tag mit himmlischem Gesang, seine Macht ausrufend also:	And the sons of God announced the fourth day In song divine, proclaiming thus His power:

CHORUS (No. 13)

CHORUS:

Die Himmel erzählen die Ehre Gottes,	The heavens are telling the glory of God,
und seiner Hände Werk zeigt an das Firmament;	The wonder of His work displays the firmament;

GABRIEL, URIEL, RAPHAEL:

Dem kommenden Tage sagt es der Tag,	To day that is coming speaks it the day,
die Nacht, die verschwand der folgenden Nacht:	The night that is gone to following night.

CHORUS:

Die Himmel erzählen die Ehre Gottes,	The heavens are telling the glory of God,
und seiner Hände Werk zeigt an das Firmament.	The wonder of His work displays the firmament.

GABRIEL, URIEL, RAPHAEL:

In alle Welt ergeht das Wort,	In all the lands resounds the word,
jedem Ohre klingend. keiner Zunge fremd:	Never unperceived, ever understood.

CHORUS:

Die Himmel erzählen die Ehre Gottes,	The heavens are telling the glory of God,
und seiner Hände Werk zeigt an das Firmament.	The wonder of His work displays the firmament.

Recitative and Chorus, "Die Himmel erzählen"

Recitativ.

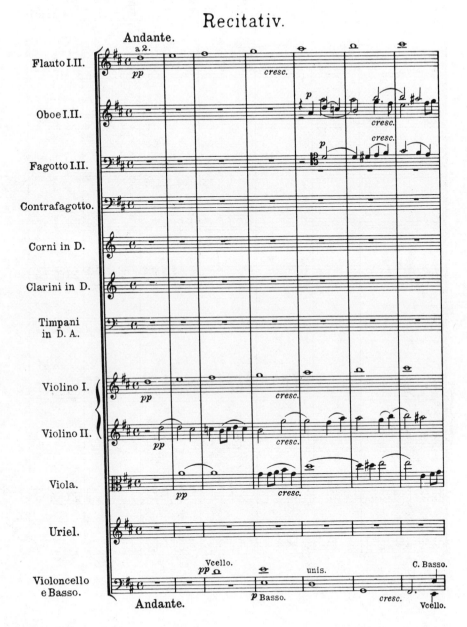

tacet.

Recit.
Uriel.

In vol-lem Glanze   steiget jetzt die Sonne strahlend auf;

C. Basso.

Vcello.

ein wonne-vol-ler Bräutigam,   ein Riese, stolz und

Chor mit Soli.

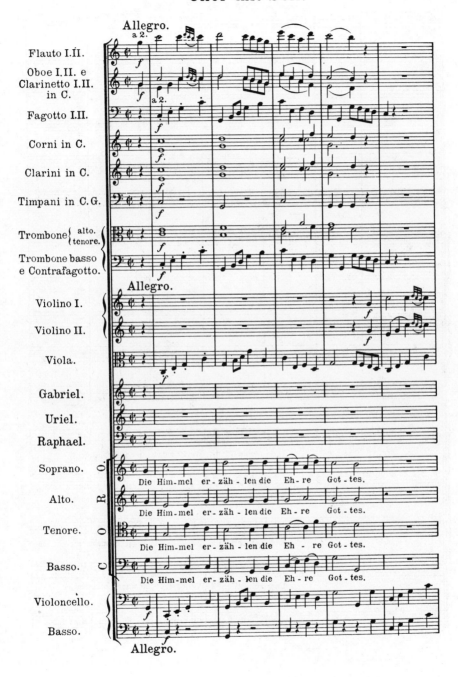

Nacht, die Nacht, die ver-schwand, der fol - genden Nacht.

Nacht, die Nacht, die ver-schwand, der fol - genden Nacht.

Nacht, die Nacht, die ver-schwand, der fol - genden Nacht.

Die Him - mel er -

Die Him - mel er -

Coro.

Die Him - mel er - zäh - len die

Die Him - mel er - zäh - len die

arco

f unis.

sei - ner Hän - de Werk   zeigt an das Fir - ma - ment,

Werk   zeigt an,   zeigt an das Fir - ma - ment,   und

Werk   zeigt an,   zeigt an das Fir - ma - ment,   und

sei - ner Hän - de Werk   zeigt an das Fir - ma - ment,

170

ment,   zeigt an,   zeigt an   das   Fir -   ma - ment.   Die

ment,   zeigt an,   zeigt an   das   Fir -   ma - ment.

Fir -   ma - ment,   das   Fir -   ma - ment.   Die Him - mel er -

ment,   zeigt an,   zeigt an   das   Fir -   ma - ment.   Die

ment,   zeigt an das Fir-ma - ment,   zeigt   an das Fir-ma - ment.

ment,   zeigt an das Fir-ma - ment,   zeigt   an das Fir-ma - ment.

ment,   zeigt an das Fir-ma - ment,   zeigt   an das Fir-ma - ment.

ment,   zeigt an das Fir-ma - ment,   zeigt   an das Fir-ma - ment.

Ende des ersten Teils.

14. String Quartet in F Major (op. 77 ii)

Composed in 1799 as the second of what evidently was planned as a set of six quartets, this famous and highly regarded piece (for Tovey it was Haydn's greatest instrumental composition) is Haydn's last completed work in this genre; thus it is also his last completed large-scale instrumental work, and as such has a certain symbolic significance, making it most fitting to include it here.

All the elements of what has come to be called the Classic style are abundantly and impressively manifested here. While the work is not overly serious in its expressive quality, elaborate procedures are nonetheless employed. The appeal is to the connoisseur and to the learned, skilled, and understanding amateur able to follow the wit of the proceedings. Here the term "wit" is used in its eighteenth-century sense of subtlety and acuteness of perception (what the Germans then called *scharfsinnig*, "sharpness of sense"). It was doubtless a piece of this kind (or one from Haydn's op. 76) that prompted Goethe's famous characterization of a string quartet as "the conversation of four knowledgeable men." The piece thus shows much the same characteristics as the Symphony in E-flat Major, except that the outgoing, popular, audience-pleasing brilliance is lacking. Apart from the fact that the Minuet comes second and the Andante third, the only feature that seems unusual is the uncommon use of key in the Trio (D-flat major) and the Andante (D major).

The first movement, Allegro moderato, employs the sonata structure, as would be expected. The homophonic principal theme is a balanced sixteen-bar period, but with a continuous unfolding of thematic material in the second eight bars. The transition (bb. 16 ff.) introduces new motives and patterns of figuration that become important later, in the development. The slower-moving secondary theme (bb. 37 ff.) uses elements of the principal theme (note especially the second violin part here). One may recognize a closing passage at b. 46. In the extended development (bb. 58 ff.) themes from the transition play the most important role, with much contrapuntal and motivic interplay and variety of register. The recapitulation (b. 115) is straightforward, with a slight extension at the end—though not really enough of one to be termed a coda.

The Minuet makes extensive use of syncopation, particularly in bb. 5–12, where a superimposed duple meter virtually obliterates the underlying 3/4. The trio, however, as if in compensation, is broadly lyrical, sonorously scored, and richly harmonized.

The genial Andante makes use of a combination in which elements of the rondo and theme-and-variations are brought together. Some complication results from the fact that the refrain (in the dominant) is also used in the first episode. In character the movement is on the light side; the refrain is attractive, with its initial two-part writing, regular phrases, dotted rhythms, and clear harmonic organization. Here is an instance where the marking "andante" truly reveals its derivation from the Italian "andare" ("to walk") and surely must not be played too slowly. As a guide to the structure, note the following: the refrain reappears in varied form at bb. 40, 74, and 105, the episodes at bb. 22 (note the use of the refrain in the dominant here at b. 27), 59, and 94, with a coda at b. 122.

In the Finale, as in the sonata-form first movement, things are simpler and more direct, yet also more brilliant. In character the whole owes much to the *polacca*, a relative of the polonaise. As is common with Haydn, the "secondary theme" (bb. 31 ff.) is really a restatement of the principal theme in the dominant. The development (b. 58) features contrapuntal elaboration and motivic work based on the theme; the recapitulation is at b. 116.

String Quartet in F Major

I

II

Menuetto. Presto, ma non troppo

III

IV

Finale. Vivace assai

3
MOZART

THE CAREER OF WOLFGANG AMADEUS MOZART (1756–91) was very different from that of his elder contemporary, Haydn. As an incredibly gifted prodigy he toured Europe in his early years (1763–73), causing a sensation wherever he appeared. But his talent had another and darker side, for he did not get on easily in the world: His manner frequently put people off, while his music was often perceived, odd as it may seem to us, as contrived, difficult, and unduly complex. Here we may refer to a letter from Melchior Grimm in Paris to Mozart's father, Leopold: Wolfgang, he says, should have "half as much talent and twice as much tact," a judgment that speaks volumes. The fateful step came in the spring of 1781, when Mozart abandoned his secure if unrewarding position in Salzburg, his birthplace, and moved to Vienna as a "free artist." At first it seemed as if he might be able to make his way, as he scored some successes with opera and piano concertos. But after 1787 things turned for the worse, and his last years brought increasing poverty and despair.

In surveying his development one may recognize first a period when his work accorded more or less with the conventions of the time (c. 1762–73), then one in which his individuality began to assert itself clearly and forcefully in a number of works (1774–81), and, finally, the period in Vienna: the years of promise (1781–86) and those of decline (1787–91).

15. Symphony No. 23 in D Major (K. 162b/181)[1]

The early works of Mozart represent his absorption of the tastes, styles, and types that prevailed around the middle of the eighteenth century, when the Italian *opera buffa* was central. What is astonishing is the way these are mastered by one so young. The symphony presented here, composed in May 1773 (one of seven composed that year) shortly after his final trip to Italy, shows the atmosphere of the *opera buffa* clearly enough. The three-movement scheme, used here with no break between movements, comes straight from the Italian operatic *sinfonia*. In other symphonies Mozart followed what seems to have been a Germanic, or at least Viennese, taste and added a minuet. This work shows a slight increase in the number of instruments routine at the time: two trumpets are added to the usual oboes, horns and strings. The symphony abounds in *buffa*-like themes, both fast and slow, which are most often cast in balanced phrases, with extensive use of melodic sequence and brilliant figuration.

The first movement, Allegro spirituoso, is in the sonata form, but without a development. There is a short coda. Right at the outset we meet with a kaleidoscopically varied succession typical of Mozart: four bars of fanfare (two two-bar units) incorporating an augmented sixth-chord (b. 3); then a triadic-motivic theme in the bass, alternating *piano* and *forte* in two-bar units, repeated while moving through different harmonies stressing the minor (G and D minor), culminating in figuration right from the *opera buffa* (bb. 19–23). A second principal theme, lyric for eight bars and syncopated for eight more, is presented before the transition (bb. 39 ff.), which features first scales and then a dotted motive. The secondary theme, with its clear antecedent-and-consequent phrase-structure (in two two-bar units), is at b. 70.

---

[1] The "K" numbers are those assigned to Mozart's works (in chronological order) in Ludwig von Koechel, *Chronologisch-thematisches Verzeichnis sämtlicher Tonwerke Wolfgang Amadé Mozarts* (Leipzig, 1862). There have been other editions of this work; preeminent among these is the third, edited by Alfred Einstein (1937), in which some changes were introduced, such that new numbers were given to some of the works. These new numbers have been retained in subsequent editions, of which the most recent is the seventh (1977). Where both numbers are given in this chapter, the first is the new number, the second the one originally used by Koechel.

The Andantino grazioso in G major is conceived like an aria, serenade, or *romanza*, in two strophes (in D major and G major), but is through-composed, with the oboe standing in for the singer. The melodic line, eminently vocal, uses simple patterns of the *siciliano* rhythm and displays great regularity of phrase-structure, with much sequential writing. To this the strings provide a conventional accompaniment. The strings also provide a ritornello at the beginning and between the two strophes, but which is omitted at the end to make way for the finale.

This, Presto assai, is a concise rondo using short-phrased themes, typical *buffa* figuration (as in the principal theme, bb. 5–8), and full chords in dotted rhythm. Finales generally are simpler in most respects than first movements. The formal arrangement of the movement is as follows: rondo (b. 270)–first episode (b. 286)–rondo (b. 310)–second episode (b. 326)–rondo (b. 350)–first episode (b. 366)–rondo (b. 390)–coda (b. 421).

Symphony No. 23 in D Major

16. Piano Concerto No. 9 in E-flat Major (K. 271)

Every once in a while there occurs a work that represents an astonishing step forward in the career of a great artist, a point at which all his forces suddenly gather together to create a work of unprecedented scope, conception, elaboration, and intensity. Such is this piano concerto, composed—rather exceptionally—for the visit to Salzburg of a French pianist, Mlle. Jeunehomme, in January 1777 (usually Mozart wrote such concertos for his own use). Up to this point Mozart's compositions had tended toward the *galant* and *opera buffa;* this was particularly true of the piano concertos. Yet he had been absorbing and assimilating influences from Haydn and, doubtless, C. P. E. Bach and was now able to produce a work that opened new vistas. Alfred Einstein refers to it quite simply as "Mozart's 'Eroica.'"

As a genre the concerto presents a peculiar situation by virtue of its long history. In Mozart's day many traditional elements required modification or reinterpretation in view of the new aesthetics, techniques, and structures that had developed in the late eighteenth century. Moreover, the respective roles of soloist and orchestra (or "tutti," as it is often called in reference to concertos) required clarification, since it would not do in most cases to have the orchestra simply provide accompaniment for the soloist. Finally, conflict between the demands of virtuosity on the one hand and for the motivic development of themes on the other constituted an important issue.

Mozart's way of resolving all this—which first appeared in this work—had an important bearing on the subsequent history of the genre, notably on Beethoven. Two main aspects were involved: First, the solo and orchestra parts were related in a subtle interplay in which the leading role shifted from one to the other and was at times shared; the role of the soloist here may be fairly described as *primus inter pares* ("first among equals"). And, second, the old ritornello structure was modified in light of the new sonata-form with its emphasis on thematic development. The chief result of this last change was in the organizational scheme of the first movement; this involved the tutti introduction, which corresponds to the old opening ritornello in a Baroque concerto or a Da Capo aria (the two being closely related). In Mozart's concertos the leading themes are often presented by the orchestra before the entrance of the soloist, who then plays it a second time with the orchestra; this arrangement is sometimes referred to as the "double exposition."

Once Mozart established all this he made no significant departures from it in subsequent concertos, except for greater elaboration in his treatment of the orchestra, notably in the use of woodwinds in the Vienna concertos of 1784 and thereafter.

While it is not possible to give here a detailed account of the concerto presented below, at least some important aspects may be pointed out. The first movement, Allegro, rather unusually introduces the soloist right away, with the principal theme's antecedent and consequent phrases divided between soloist and tutti. Then the tutti exposition proceeds with a profusion of contrasting thematic elements; the stress here is on motivic development (especially in bb. 14–22). After the reentrance of the soloist (b. 56), first with new material (to set it off, not unlike the entrance of a main character in an opera), the whole exposition is toured again, but with extended passages featuring figuration (bb. 69–82, for instance) and accompaniment by motives from the principal theme. The development (bb. 148 ff.) centers around the two principal themes, again with much motivic work. In the recapitulation (bb. 196 ff.), for the presentation of the first principal theme the earlier roles of soloist and tutti are exchanged. The cadenza, where the soloist was to improvise on the main themes, comes at b. 292.

The Andantino, in C minor, an unexpectedly serious movement, explicitly draws on operatic elements; the whole may be regarded as a kind of aria. Structurally we find the sonata form with the development or middle section at b. 53 and the recapitulation at b. 76; the cadenza is at b. 122. As in an aria, the orchestra begins, here muted; one is surprised to note the use of canon between the violins. The last four bars of this orchestral passage, with short phrases and a "sob" figure of a descending semitone, resemble an operatic recitative, complete with the conventional melodic cadence (bb. 12–16). The combination of intense expression and elaboration of technique is symbolic of the work as a whole.

The finale uses, as is customary in concertos, the rondo scheme exhibiting great brilliance in the figurative elements used in the themes. Yet the rondo also incorporates passages of a developmental character. Most noteworthy is the appearance of a complete minuet, in full rounded-binary form, during the second episode. The full scheme of the movement is: rondo—first episode (b. 82)—rondo (b. 150; preceded by a cadenza)—second episode (b. 192, a development; and b. 233, the minuet)—rondo (b. 304)—development (b. 320)—first episode (b. 355)—rondo (b. 424).

The concerto in general occupies a position of central importance in Mozart's work; since it constituted a most important item in public concerts,

Mozart laid great stress on it during the earlier part of his stay in Vienna.[1] In a letter to his father he gave a sharp description of the three concertos composed in 1782, one which applies equally to his others:

> Now these concertos are the middle thing between too hard and too easy—very brilliant—pleasing to the ear. Natural, without becoming empty—also here and there connoisseurs alone can find satisfaction, but in such a way that those who are not connoisseurs will have to be satisfied with it without knowing why.[2]

---

[1] For a representative example of these Vienna concertos, see Concerto No. 23 in A major (K. 488); this can be found in Godwin, *Schirmer Scores*, No. 58, pp. 754–807.

[2] Letter of 28 December 1782; translation by F. E. K.

Piano Concerto No. 9 in E-flat Major

Andantino.

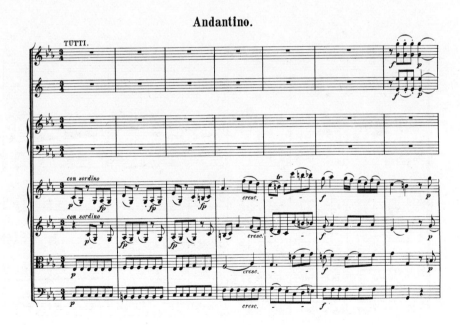

Rondo.

Menuetto.

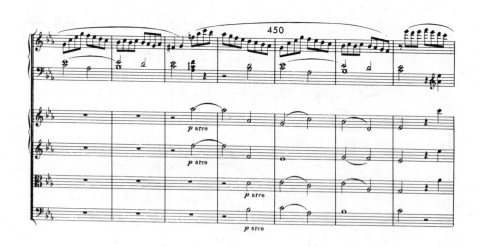

17. Selections from *Die Entführung aus dem Serail* ["The Abduction from the Harem," K. 384]: Aria, "Solche hergelauf'ne Laffen"; Recitative and Aria, "O wie ängstlich"; Trio, Finale, Act I

This opera—more correctly, *Singspiel* [1]—was the central work of Mozart's first year in Vienna, 1781–2. Its success was such as to make it seem likely that his adventurous decision to leave Salzburg and come to Vienna would turn out favorably. Briefly, this operatic work may be described as a "Turkish rescue-opera": Belmonte and his servant Pedrillo set out to rescue Constanze, who has been captured by the despot Selim Pascha, and to do this must outwit Osmin, the eunuch in charge of the harem.

While composing this work in the fall of 1781 Mozart expressed himself on the aesthetics of opera, as it were, in several letters to his father Leopold. The most interesting of these letters is the one dated 26 September, in which individual numbers in the work are described in some detail. Our musical examples have been chosen to correspond with what he discussed in this letter.

It is evident that Mozart attached particular importance to the character Osmin, the villainous and comic eunuch. The discussion of Osmin's rage-aria, "Solche hergelauf'ne Laffen" (No. 3 in the opera) is comprehensive and revealing.

> The rage of Osmin will be rendered comic . . . as the Turkish music is thus brought in. [2]

---

[1] A *Singspiel* was a musico-dramatic work in German in which musical numbers were separated by spoken dialogue (instead of *recitativo secco*), usually comic: thus, an eighteenth-century German version of our modern musical comedy.

[2] For this effect a large battery of percussion instruments (triangle, cymbals, tambourines, bass drum, etc.) was used, as in a Janissary band. Other prominent works using "Turkish" music are Haydn's Symphony No. 100 in G major ("The Military") and Beethoven's Symphony No. 9 in D minor (in the finale).

394

The tempo, Mozart goes on, must increase in keeping with Osmin's rage, and

> then—when one thinks the aria is at its end, the Allegro assai in quite another
> tempo and in another key must make a splendid effect; for a man who is in
> such a rage oversteps all moderation, measure, and bounds; he does not know
> himself—so the music must not [know itself]; although the utmost passion,
> violent or not, must never be pushed so far as the disgusting, and music even
> in the most awful places must not offend the ear, but give pleasure; that is,
> music must always remain music; so I have chosen no foreign key to the F
> [the main key], but a consonant one, not however the nearest D minor but
> the further A minor.[3]

In the same vein, in a letter of 13 October Mozart says, "in an opera the poetry
must be the obedient daughter of the music," a view contrasting with that
of Gluck (see above, p. 62).

What Mozart says in the letter is clear enough in the aria itself. The first
main section, an Allegro con brio in F major which presents Osmin's angry
denunciation of Belmonte and Pedrillo, is in two parts, the second paralleling
the first but with different key relations. Each of these parts is divided itself
into two parts, the second marked Allegro (immediately following the short
Adagio). Osmin's part is characterized by repeated notes, chromatic scale seg-
ments, and wide leaps; in the Allegro, short phrases based on standard patterns
of figuration predominate. There then follows a coda in the *parlante* vein so
common in eighteenth-century comic opera.[4] This is, in Mozart's words, "when
one thinks the aria is at its end." Then, after a short interchange of spoken
dialogue (often omitted in performance), comes the Allegro assai in A minor,
complete with the piccolo, cymbals (*piatti*), and bass drum (*tamburo grande*)
associated with Turkish music, thus making Mozart's "splendid effect"; again
the *parlante* style is employed.

Of Belmonte's aria, "O wie ängstlich," we read:

> the beating, loving heart—two violins in octaves . . . One sees the swelling
> breast heave—which is expressed by a crescendo—one hears the whispering
> and sighing—which is given by the first violins with mutes and a flute in unison.[5]

In each section the character of the music changes in accordance with the
text, the parts specified above by Mozart being clearly recognizable: the beat-

---

[3] Translation by W. J. Turner, *Mozart: the Man and His Works* (New York, 1938), pp.
307–8). For the full text of the letter, see *The Letters of Mozart and His Family*, translated and edited by Emily Anderson, 2nd edition (New York, 1966), II, pp. 769–70 (No.
426).

[4] Parlante is a type of melodic writing intended to resemble speech to some extent; characterized by a fast tempo, it features inconsequential melodic material in the vocal parts
(repeated notes and triadic figures usually in short phrases) so that the figuration in the
orchestra assumes relatively greater interest. See the fine discussion in Joseph Kerman,
Opera as Drama (New York, 1956), pp. 136–9, which, while it deals primarily with Verdi,
is applicable here.

[5] From Turner. See Note 3.

ing, loving heart (bb. 9 ff.), the heaving of the swelling breast (bb. 33 ff.), and the whispering and sighing (bb. 46 ff.). Yet one may wonder whether the beating, loving heart is expressed by the violins in octaves, as Mozart said, or by the short phrases of slurred pairs of notes interrupted by brief rests.

The Trio at the end of Act I may be explained by referring to the convention of the finale in an opera—a series of connected ensembles (recitative is usually excluded, except for very short passages) in which the rapid twists of the plot are graphically realized in the music: As the number of characters on the stage increases, so does the tempo of the music. This trio provides a good illustration of much of this. Mozart says of it:

> As the text permits I have written it rather well for three voices. Then begins immediately the major pianissimo, which must go very fast, and this will make a really good row—and that is everything desirable in the finale of a first act —the more noise the better; the shorter the better, so that the audience does not cool off in its clapping.[6]

In the main section we again find a two-part scheme, except that here there is an interlude of nineteen bars between parts. First, Osmin rounds up the protesting Belmonte and Pedrillo; then they give in to his prodding; and finally, presumably after a little stage business, he continues with his threats and they with their giving in. This last part, commencing in E-flat, shows the differentiation in melodic style—here between Osmin on the one hand and Belmonte and Pedrillo on the other—that was to assume cardinal importance in operatic ensembles in times to come (see below, Number 22, "Selections from *Don Giovanni*"—"Minuet Scene" and "Trio, 'Ah, taci . . .'"—and Number 28, "Trio from *Fidelio*"). There then follows the Allegro assai in C major (what Mozart called "the major *pianissimo*," a description not entirely borne out by the score as it stands), in which the faster tempo is quickened still more by having triplets replace the eighth-note duplets. Throughout, elements of the *buffa* style are prominent: the short phrases (often triadic or with repeated notes) characteristic of the *parlante*, and typical *buffa* figurations in the orchestra (e.g., bb. 26 ff., first violins).

Texts and Translation [7]

ARIA FOR OSMIN

Solche hergelauf'ne Laffen,	Such fops who come running in here,
die nur nach den Weibern gaffen,	Who do nothing but chase women—
mag ich vor den Teufel nicht;	By the Devil! I can't stand them;

[6] From Turner. See Note 3.
[7] Translation by F. E. K.

denn ihr ganzes Tun und Lassen ist:
uns auf den Dienst zu passen,
doch mich trügt kein solch Gesicht.

Eure Tücken, eure Ränke,
eure Finten, eure Schwänke,
sind mir ganz bekannt;

mich zu hintergehen
müsst ihr früh aufstehen;
ich hab' auch Verstand.

Drum, beim Barte des Propheten!

ich studiere Tag und Nacht,
ruh' nicht bis ich dich seh' tödten,

nimm du wie du willst in Acht.

Erst geköpft, dann gehangen,
dann gespiesst auf heissen Stangen,
dann verbrannt, dann gebunden
und getaucht; zuletzt geschunden.

For your only interest is:
To watch us as we work,
Yet you do not fool me.

Your pranks, your plots,
Your feints, your jests,
Are all well known to me;

If you want to get around me
You will have to get up early;
I know what's going on.

Therefore, by the beard of the
prophet!

I stay awake day and night,
I'll not rest till I see you killed,

Be as careful as you like.

First beheaded, then hung up,
Then impaled on hot rods,
Then burned, then tied up
And ducked in water; finally thrown
out.

Aria for Belmonte
Recitative

Konstanze, dich wiederzusehen, dich!

Constance, if only to see you—you—
again!

Aria

O wie ängstlich, o wie feurig
klopft mein liebevolles Herz!
Und des Wiedersehens Zähre
lohnt der Trennung bangen Schmerz.

Nun zittr' ich und wanke,
nun zag' ich und schwanke;
es hebt sich die schwellende Brust!—

Ist das ihr Lispeln?
Es wird mir so bange!—
War das ihr Seufzen?
Es glüht mir die Wange!
Täuscht mich die Liebe?
War es ein Traum?

O how anxiously, how full of ardor
Beats my heart so full of love!
And the tears at reunion
Reward the anxious pain of separation.

Now I'm shivering and wavering,
Now I'm hesitant and faltering;
My swelling breast heaves!—

Is that her whispering?
I'm so afraid!—
Was that her sighing?
My cheeks are blushing!
Does love deceive me?
Was that a dream?

Trio from Finale, Act I

OSMIN:

Marsch! Marsch! Marsch! Trollt euch fort!	March, march march! toddle along now!
Sonst soll die Bastonade	Or else the bastinade
Euch gleich zu Diensten stehn!	Will go to work on you.

BELMONTE AND PEDRILLO:

Ei, ei! Das wär' ja schade,	Oh, oh, it would be a shame
Mit uns so umzugehn!	To treat us that way!

OSMIN:

Kommt nur nicht näher.	Just don't come any closer.

BELMONTE AND PEDRILLO:

Weg von der Türe.	Get away from the door.

OSMIN:

Sonst schlag' ich drein.	Or I'll shove you in.

BELMONTE AND PEDRILLO:

Wir gehn hinein!	We're going.

OSMIN:

Marsch fort! Ich schlage drein!	March on! I'll push you in.

BELMONTE UND PEDRILLO:

Platz, fort! Wir gehn hinein!	Make way! We're going in.

Aria (*Osmin*), "Solche hergelauf'ne Laffen"

uns auf den Dienst zu passen, uns auf den Dienst zu passen, doch mich trägt kein solch Ge_

ad libitum.

sicht, doch mich trägt kein solch Ge_sicht. Eure Tü_cken, eu_re Ränke, eu_re Fin_ten, eu_re

30   Adagio.   Allegro.

Schwänke sind mir ganz bekannt, sind mir ganz bekannt, sind mir ganz bekannt, ganz bekannt, sind mir ganz be_

kannt; mich zu hin-ter-gehen müsst ihr früh auf-stehen, müsst ihr früh auf-ste-hen;

ich hab' auch Ver-stand, ich hab' auch Ver-stand, ich hab' auch Ver-stand, ich! ich hab' auch Ver-

stand. Sol-che her-ge-lauf'ne Laf — — — — — — fen,

die nur nach den Weibern gaf _ fen, mag ich vor den Teu _ fel nicht, mag ich vor den Teufel

nicht, mag ich vor den Teu_fel nicht; denn ihr ganzes Thun und Lassen ist: uns auf den Dienst zu

passen, uns auf den Dienst zu passen, doch mich trägt kein solch Ge_sicht, doch mich

Ver _ _ stand, ich hab' auch Ver _ stand. Drum, beim Barte des Pro_

phe_ten! ich stu _ di _ re Tag und Nacht, ruh' nicht bis ich dich seh' tö _ dten, nimm dich wie du willst in

Acht, drum, beim Bar _ te des Pro _ phe _ ten, ich stu _ di _ re Tag und Nacht, ruh' nicht bis ich dich seh'

Recitative and Aria (*Belmonte*), "O wie ängstlich"

ban - - gen Schmerz; schon zittr'ich und wanke, schon zag'ich und schwanke. schon zag' ich und

schwan-ke, es hebt sich die schwel_len_de Brust, es hebt sich die schwel_len_de

War das ihr Seuf_zen? Es glüht mir die Wan ge! Täuscht mich die Lie be, war es ein

Traum? täuscht mich die Lie be, war es ein Traum? täuscht mich die Lie be, war es ein

Traum? O wie ängstlich, o wie feurig, klopft mein lie - be - vol - les Herz, klopft mein

lie - be - vol - les Herz, klopft mein lie - be - vol - - - - - - - - - - - les

feu-rig, klopft mein lie_be_vol_les Herz, klopft mein lie-be-vol_les Herz, klopft mein

lie_be_vol_les Herz! Schon zittr' ich und wan_ke, schon zag' ich und schwanke, o wie

Trio, Finale, Act I (*Osmin, Belmonte, Pedrillo*)

18.   String Quartet in G Major (K. 387)

Mozart's evolution as a serious quartet composer in its earlier phase was to a large extent dependent upon Haydn. In 1773, under the impact of Haydn's six op. 20 quartets, he produced six of his own (K. 168–173) in which the external aspects of Haydn's achievement are imitated. A decade or so later, during which time neither composed any quartets, Haydn's op. 33 (another set of six) prompted Mozart in the years 1782–5 to compose a set which he himself described as "the fruit of a long and laborious work," and which he dedicated to the older composer, giving him the original fair copy and assigning him all rights to the pieces—a rare homage.[1] By this time Mozart had developed as a composer to the point where he was no longer overwhelmed by Haydn, but could use Haydn's accomplishments as a stimulus for his own work.

While the first of this set of six provides our example, the wealth and variety exhibited throughout is such that no one work can really stand for all. Composed in 1782, the quartet follows the four-movement scheme that had become standard for the genre, except that the minuet is placed second and the slow movement, Andante cantabile in F major, comes third. Among the noteworthy features of the first movement are the lyric nature of the principal theme, lightly spiced with incidental chromaticisms (which needless to say are important elsewhere, as in bb. 15–20); the nicely contrasting, *galant* secondary theme (bb. 24 ff.) and the brilliant closing passage (bb. 38 ff.); and in the development, the free spinning-out from the principal theme, which leads to a passage of new figuration, whereafter elements from the closing passage are brought in. The recapitulation is at b. 107.

Chromaticism and counterpoint are important in the Minuet (note the syncopations), whereas the Trio, in G minor, balances its gruff beginning with smooth lyricism later.

The serious Andante cantabile, much like an aria, is cast in the large binary

---

[1] The six quartets in question are: the G Major (K. 387), D Minor (K. 417b/421), E-flat Major (K. 421b/428), B-flat Major (K. 458, "The Hunt"), A Major (K. 464) and C Major (K. 465, "The Dissonant").

arrangement, the first part resembling an exposition, the second (bb. 51 ff.) a recapitulation. The only real difference between these parts comes right at the end (although one passage is notably extended—compare bb. 58–69 with 7–14). Here the melodic value of the themes themselves is paramount, along with the coloristic use of timbre and modulation, as in the "disconsolate" (as Einstein would say) secondary theme (bb. 25 ff.).

In the finale the bright quality is restored and we meet with one of Mozart's earlier incorporations of fugal passages into a movement using the sonata structure. Not only is the principal theme fugal, but the subject, in whole notes and having as countersubject a series of suspensions, smacks of the counterpoint book. Once the fugal exposition has been completed, the brilliant-galant style takes over, as figuration provides the thematic material (bb. 17 ff.)—although there is still some elaboration of part-writing in what ensues (bb. 31 ff.). In the transition (bb. 51 ff.), however, the fugal writing returns, and the principal theme is reintroduced in contrapuntal combination with the new thematic element (bb. 69–84). Relief comes with the secondary theme (b. 91 ff.), simple and bright. This sudden shift of mood—here, from the learned to the galant—is salient in Mozart's art. The development uses the principal theme, combining it with a chromatic scale-passage and then with a repeated-note figure; a chromatic passage based on this repeated-note figure leads to the recapitulation (b. 175), from which the principal theme has been eliminated. A coda (b. 268) resembles the development, but goes on to present the principal theme in stretto in all parts, as climax near the end (bb. 282–8).

String Quartet in G Major

MINUETTO.
Allegro.

19. Symphony No. 38 in D Major (*Prague*, K. 504)

During the years in Vienna, Mozart, although composing fewer symphonies than before, began conceiving of this genre as grander and more important than he had previously thought it. We find two large works right at the start of his Vienna years, when he was attempting to establish himself as a public performer: the brilliant symphonies in D major (K. 385, "Haffner") and C major (K. 425, "Linz") of 1782 and 1783 respectively. At this time he also wrote a slow introduction for a symphony by Michael Haydn (K. 425a/444). Thereafter the symphony lost ground in his output as he turned to the piano concerto, opera, and chamber music. However, three years later, in 1786, he returned to the symphony, composing the one in D major (K. 504, "Prague") selected here. Two years later (in the summer of 1788) he composed the famous final set of three—the symphonies in E-flat (K. 543), G minor (K. 550) and C major (K. 551, "Jupiter")—with which he may have thought of taking up concertizing once again, a plan he did not fulfill.

The Symphony in D Major, completed early in December 1786, was first performed at a concert in Prague on 19 January 1787, where Mozart had gone to be present at performances of *The Marriage of Figaro*, given there with great success. The symphony indeed has much of the *opera buffa* about it, especially in the return to the three-movement formal scheme and in the pervasive aura of variety, contrast, and brilliance. Here mercurial changes from one character or topic to another reach an apogee even for Mozart.

All three movements make use of the sonata structure. The first presents the most variety. It commences with a slow introduction which moves from the portentous (briefly anticipating the entrance of the statue, and the overture, in *Don Giovanni*) to expressive lyricism. In the Allegro we get, in quick succession, lyricism (as in bb. 37–40 and 45–50), brilliant figuration (as in bb. 55–70), and contrapuntal part-writing (as in bb. 71–86) punctuated by short fanfares (as in b. 43). The secondary theme, here a true "relief" theme, appears at bb. 97 ff. Much of all this is prominent in the development (bb. 143 ff.), especially the use of counterpoint, where a new motive (leaping up an octave and then descending stepwise) is combined with the principal theme (as in bb. 156 ff.). There is a sort of false recapitulation at b. 189; in the real recapitulation (bb. 208 ff.), the brilliantly effective close (especially bb. 282–96) is especially engaging.

In the Andante in G major, the first principal theme has a distinct resemblance to the aria "Dalla sua pace," to be composed later for the Viennese performances of *Don Giovanni*. It and the closing theme (bb. 54 ff.) are important in the development (bb. 58 ff.), the latter at the beginning, which makes for greater continuity by minimizing contrast between the sections. The recapitulation starts at b. 94.

As a finale there is a brilliant Presto of great rhythmic exhilaration and variegated instrumentation, in which the woodwinds are frequently pitted in alternation with the strings (as in the secondary theme, bb. 66 ff.). The development begins at b. 152 and the recapitulation at b. 216, with an important departure from the exposition, between b. 228 and 244.

Symphony No. 38 in D Major (*Prague*)

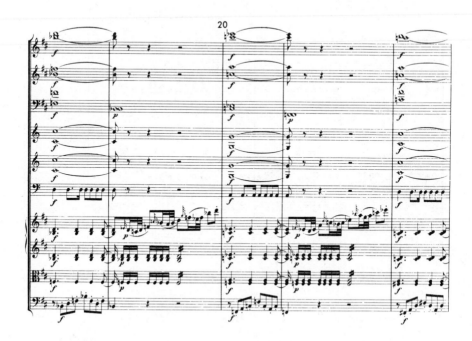

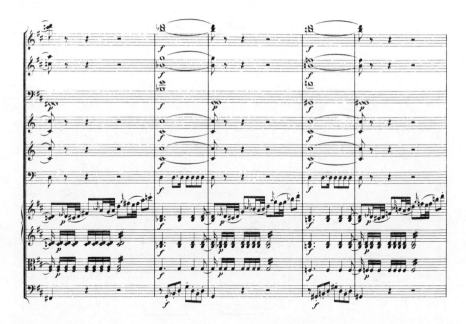

100

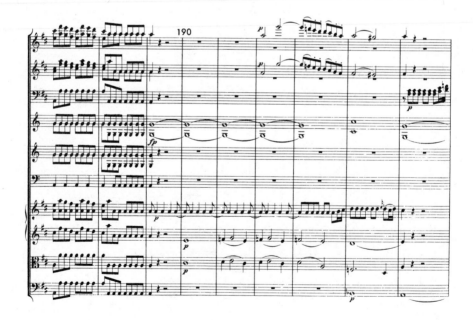

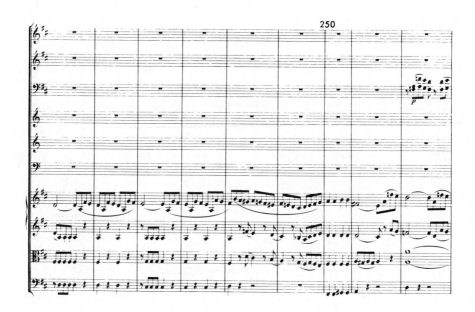

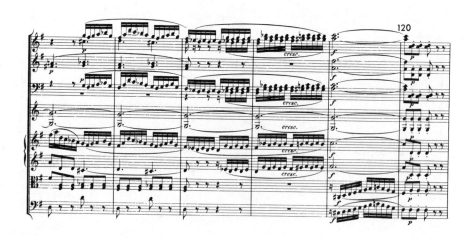

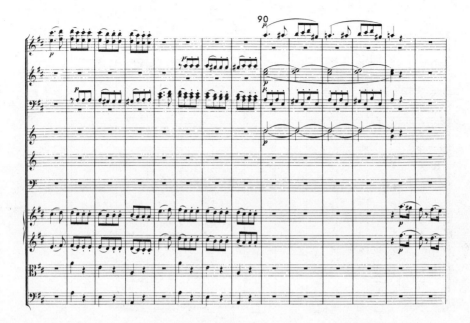

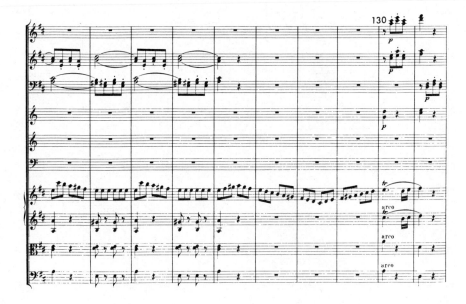

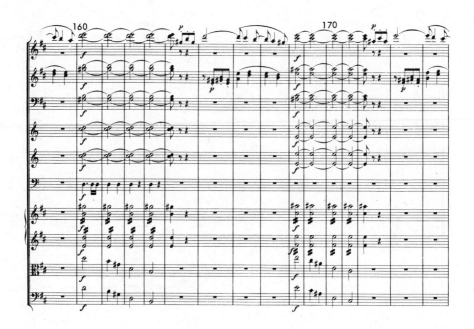

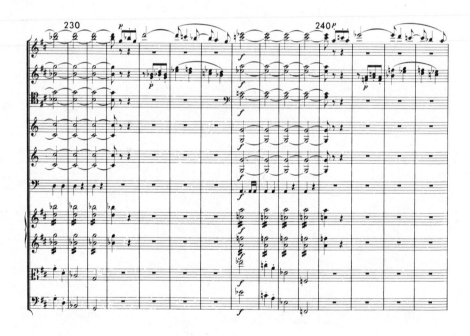

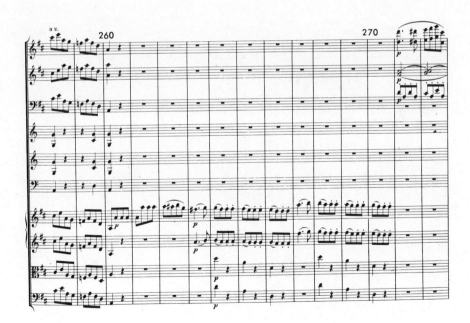

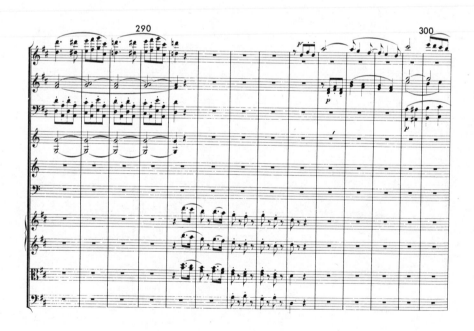

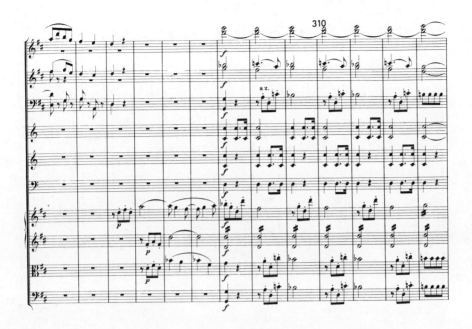

20. String Quintet in G Minor (K. 516)

After the completion of the six great quartets dedicated to Haydn, Mozart turned his attention to another genre of string ensemble music without piano —the quintet, here a quartet with second viola. This category of composition, fashionable in the Viennese and South German repertory of the time, usually conformed to the *galant* taste. Mozart, however, changed this, endowing his works in the genre with powerful expression, complex part-writing, and elaborate harmonies, thus taking advantage of the increased possibilities for sonority and part-writing afforded by the second viola. From many points of view these works may be regarded as the pinnacle of his work in instrumental music.

Apart from an early and wholly *galant* effort of 1773 in B-flat major (K. 174), Mozart took up the genre in the spring of 1787 with two works of radically contrasting character, one in C major (K. 515), the other in G minor (K. 516).[1] He also produced a third in C minor (K. 516b/406), which is in fact the transcription of a Serenade for woodwinds (K. 384a/388). Later he composed two more, one in D major (K. 593) in 1790 and the other in E-flat major (K. 618) in 1791, one of his very last works.

The affection prevailing in the Quintet in G Minor, one long associated with that key, may be described as passionate sorrow; it is somewhat like that in the Largo of Haydn's Quartet in G Major, op. 33 v (discussed above, pp. 134 ff.). This character is manifested by the lyrical nature of the themes, chromaticism in melody and harmony, and effective use of changes in dynamics (which dominate the work). Relief of a sort comes in the G major Trio of the Minuet, in the slow movement (in E-flat major), and in the finale. A few aspects of this extraordinary work are detailed.

The piece is cast in the four-movement structure, by now standard for serious instrumental compositions. In the first movement, Allegro, written in sonata structure with a dramatic coda, we find the greatest weight, as would

---

[1] The frequency with which works so contrasting in character are composed either simultaneously or consecutively is striking. Some examples: in Mozart, the piano concertos in D minor (K. 466) and C major (K. 467) and the famous symphonies in G minor (K. 550) and C major (K. 551, "Jupiter"); in Beethoven, the fifth and sixth symphonies (op. 67 and op. 68 respectively).

be expected. The principal theme, as once lyric, triadic and motivic, with chromatic inflections, starts in a relatively high register, is repeated in a lower (an illustration of the possibilities afforded by the quintet medium), and concluded by the entire ensemble together. The contrasting theme (it brings little relief) appears immediately after (bb. 29 ff.) in the transition passage, so that firm establishment of the secondary key is delayed until near the end of the exposition (b. 64). The short but intense development (bb. 94 ff.) is based mainly on this contrasting theme, treated both motivically and in contrapuntal imitation; the recapitulation is at b. 133. There is a dramatic coda (bb. 231 ff.).

The Minuet continues in much the same spirit, emphasizing chromaticsm, changes in dynamics, and syncopated accentuations, while the Trio, in a chromatically ambivalent G major, brings a little (but not much) lightness to the proceedings.

The Andante, in E-flat major, is a very serious, *con sordino*, aria-like piece cast in the large binary structure, with what may be called an exposition followed by a recapitulation (bb. 38 ff.). Particularly expressive is the passage that first appears in B-flat minor (bb. 18–22).

The concluding rondo is linked to the slow movement by a deeply expressive slow introduction in G minor, an arioso-like, chromatically inflected solo for the first violin, with the violoncello a strong counter-voice. The other instruments maintain a subdued, constantly-moving accompaniment, using for the most part simple harmonies (except at the climax, bb. 19–29), and stressing changes between minor and major. The rondo, which brings a *lieto fine* to this intensely passionate and serious composition, includes passages in the nature of a development, along with the full rondo scheme of refrains and couplets. The formal scheme may be represented as follows:

Bar
38	Refrain 1; rounded-binary form, in G major
59	Refrain 2; also rounded-binary form, in G major
82	Transition (a development, based on Refrain 2)
105	Episode or Couplet 1, in D major
147	Refrain 1, in G major
178	Episode or Couplet 2; in rounded-binary form, in C major
193	Transition (development, based on Refrain 2)
232	Episode or Couplet 1
281	Refrain 1
306	Refrain 2 (shortened)
311	Coda

String Quintet in G Minor

MINUETTO.
Allegretto.

Trio.

Adagio ma non troppo.

21.   Minuet from *Ein musikalischer Spass*
["A Musical Joke," K. 522]

Frequently one is forcefully struck by Mozart's extraordinary sense of humor. His letters are full of word-plays and puns which are often in more than one language, occasionally unprintable, and usually untranslatable, with their reshuffled syntactical elements, anagrams, and rimes. He was known to introduce himself as "Mr. Trazom" or "Mr. Romatz." His comments about and (all too frequent) to his colleagues were presumably couched in the same pithy language.

While countless examples of this may be found in his music, by all odds the most striking is this Serenade or Divertimento in F major for string quartet and horns, written late in the spring of 1787. This four-movement work, the occasion for which is unknown, ostensibly satirizes incompetent musicians, and while it was given the title, "The Village Musicians," it is by no means clear that Mozart's targets were exclusively or even primarily rural. The transgressions are numerous; they involve for the most part sudden, improper changes and mixtures of styles, with awkward transitions from one to the other, as well as poor part-writing (often with excessive doubling) and incorrect harmonies (notably the end of the whole piece).

A good illustration of all this is provided by the second movement, the Minuet and Trio. In the first part of the Minuet we note the use of plain melodic sequence, the too-sudden introduction of triplets and dotted rhythms in the horns, and the equally poorly-prepared switch to the legato style in a passage relying excessively on parallel thirds. The second part moves from pomposity to the extraordinary passage (bb. 16–20) where the horns chromatically part company with the rest of the ensemble, only to regroup valiantly for the repeat of the first part (b. 20) as if nothing had happened. The horns in this dissonant passage are appropriately marked "dolce." The Trio features long, pointless figurative lines that lead nowhere, the sudden and awkward change at bb. 47–8, and the unprepared introduction of concerto-like material (bb. 55 ff.). Such stylistic mixtures constitute most of the humor of the piece.

We do not know, as said earlier, for what occasion or purpose Mozart composed this piece, which Einstein calls "a negative key to Mozart's aesthetics" —in short, a lesson in how not to compose. But Einstein may be right in explaining the more familiar Serenade in G Major (K. 525), *Eine kleine Nachtmusik* (composed several weeks later), as Mozart's lesson on how to do it right.

Minuet from *Ein musikalischer Spass* ["A Musical Joke"]

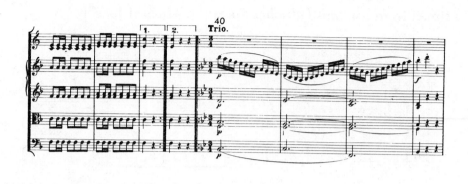

Dal segno

22. Selections from *Don Giovanni* (K. 527):
Aria, "Madamina, il catalogo";
Recitative and Aria, "Or sai chi l'onore";
Excerpt ("Minuet Scene"), from Finale,
Act I; Trio, "Ah! taci, ingiusto core";
Aria, "Il mio tesoro"

As the *opera buffa* came to dominate the repertory after the middle of the eighteenth century, the genre increased its scope to the extent that it came to include large-scale works embracing serious as well as comic elements. Carlo Goldoni (1707–93), a leading Italian playwright and librettist, expressly designated certain roles in an *opera buffa* as serious (*parti serie*), and others as comic (*parti buffe*). While this convention had been drawn upon by Mozart before, most notably in *The Marriage of Figaro*, probably its decisive appearance is in *Don Giovanni* (K. 527).

The subject-matter of this opera is the old Spanish story of the profligate lover, Don Juan, whose amorous escapades are finally ended by his encounter with the statue of the Commander, the slain father of one of his victims, whom he invites to dine with him. Hence the descriptive subtitles: *Il dissoluto punito* ("The Dissolute One Punished") and *Il convitato di pietro* or *le festin de pierre* (known in English as "The Stone Guest"). In time other elements joined those of the comic and of horror and the supernatural already present in the tale, notably the comic servant and the revenge of one of Don Juan's victims. It was usually presented at the time as an improvised, crude sort of popular entertainment, on the order of an early Frankenstein movie (in Italy known as a *commedia di cappa e spada*—"cloak and dagger comedy"). However, it also attracted the attention of more serious writers such as Molière and even

Goldoni; Gluck wrote a ballet on the subject in 1761, and in 1787, just before Mozart and his librettist Lorenzo Da Ponte set to work, an Italian opera on the subject by Gazzaniga was performed in Vienna with some success. In this universal aspect, moving from low comedy to high entertainment, the Don Juan story resembles that of Faust.

In Mozart's version, composed for and first performed in Prague on 29 October 1787, the story is relatively simple and the action, except for some episodes in Act II, moves rapidly and directly. We follow the Don's assault on Anna, the intervention of her father, the Commander, and the duel which results in his death, in an atmosphere of horror; the entrance of Elvira, the Don's abandoned wife, and Leporello's comic recounting of the Don's amorous escapades; the Don's pursuit of the peasant girl, Zerlina; Anna's recognition of the Don as her seducer and the start of her quest for vengeance; the great masked ball scene (Finale Act I), where the Don and Leporello barely escape; the episodic Act II, with the Don and Leporello exchanging cloaks and the comic situations which result; the return of the atmosphere of horror in the graveyard scene, when the Commander's statue speaks and the Don invites him to dinner; and finally, the culminating banquet scene, where festivity turns to horror as the statue arrives and exacts full vengeance on the unrepentant Don. The final sextet, which restores the atmosphere of *opera buffa*, was not part of the original version; it was added for the production in Vienna.

Particularly noteworthy is the way musical styles, types, and forms are used for characterization. While the noble characters, Anna, Elvira, Ottavio, and the Commander all use forms from the *opera seria*, the others, Leporello, Zerlina, and Masetto (Zerlina's fiancé), use the simpler and popular types from the *opera buffa*. The Don, however, moves easily among the various styles and types, since change and adaptability are very much the seducer's part.

The five selections that follow show these different aspects of the work.

ARIA (LEPORELLO), "MADAMINA, IL CATALOGO"

This famous aria (No. 4 in the opera, known as the "Catalogue Aria"), thoroughly in *buffa* style, presents Leporello's description of the Don's almost numberless amorous conquests. The key, D major, not only is common in comic operas, but in this work is, as Ratner says, associated with the Don's "wordly aspect, status, arrogance, and brilliance." The aria is in two sections: In the first, where the enumeration of his conquests is given, the thematic interest is in the orchestra, while Leporello's part remains melodically neutral, all of which is typical of the *parlante* (except for the clincher, his report that in Spain there have been 1003 such affairs—bb. 28–36 and 64–71). The second part adopts the rhythm and tempo of the minuet, the aristocratic court dance *par excellence* (bb. 85 ff.), as Leporello proceeds to describe the Don's conquests. Pictorial touches abound throughout the aria.

Text and translation

Madamina, il catalogo è questo	Pretty lady, this is the catalogue
Delle belle, che amò il padron mio;	Of the fair ladies my master has loved!
Un catalogo egli è, che ho fatto io.	It's a catalogue I made myself.
Osservate, leggete con me.	Observe, read with me.
In Italia seicento e quaranta,	In Italy six hundred and forty,
In Almagna duecento e trentuna,	In Germany two hundred and thirty,
Cento in Francia, in Turchia	A hundred in France, in Turkey
novantuna,	ninety-one,
Ma in Ispagna son già mille e tre!	But in Spain there are already one
	thousand and three!

V'han fra queste contadine,	Amongst these there are peasant girls,
Cameriere, cittadine,	Chambermaids, townswomen;
V'han contesse, baronesse,	There are countesses, baronesses,
Marchesine, principesse,	Marchionesses, princesses,
E v'han donne d'ogni grado,	And there are women of every degree,
D'ogni forma, d'ogni età.	Every shape, every age.
In Italia seicento e quaranta, *etc.*	In Italy six hundred and forty, *etc.*

Nella bionda egli ha l'usanza	In the blonde he is accustomed
Di lodarla la gentilezza;	To praise her kindness;
Nella bruna la constanza;	In the brunette her constancy;
Nella bianca la dolcezza;	In the white-haired her sweetness;
Vuol d'inverno la grassotta,	In the winter he wants a plump one,
Vuol d'estate la magrotta;	In summer a slim one;
È la grande maestosa,	The tall one is stately,
La piccina è ognor vezzosa;	The small one is always charming;
Delle vecchie fa conquista	He makes a conquest of the old ones
Pel piacer di porle in lista.	For the pleasure of putting them on
	the list.

Sua passion predominante	His dominant passion
È la giovin principiante.	Is the young beginner.
Non si picca se sia ricca,	He doesn't care a fig if she's rich,
Se sia brutta, se sia bella,	If she's ugly, if she's pretty,
Se sia ricca, brutta,	If she's rich, ugly,
Se sia bella;	If she's pretty;
Purchè porti la gonella,	So long as she wears a skirt,
Voi sapete quel che fa!	You know what he does!

Aria (*Leporello*), "Madamina, il catalogo"

In I _ talia sei cento e qua_ranta,   in Al _ magna due cento e trent
In I _ talien sechshundert und vierzig,   hier in Deutschland zweihundert und

u_na,   cen_to in Francia, in Turchia novant' u_na, ma in I_spagna, main I_spagna son
neune,   da in Frankreich nur hundert und ei_ne, doch, doch in Spanien, doch in Spanien sind

già mille e tre, mille e tre, mille e tre. V'han fra que_ste con_ta_di_ne,
schon tausenddrei, tausenddrei, tausenddrei. Das sind schmucke Kammerkätzchen,

ca_me_rie_re, cit_ta_ di_ne, v'han contesse, baro_nesse, marchesane, princi_pes_se, e v'han donne d'ogni
und hier nette Bürgerschätzchen, die_se Anzahl Baro_nessen, Ehrendamen und Comtessen, jeden Standes, jeden

grado, d'ogni forma, d'ogni e_tà, d'ogni   for_ma, d'ogni e_tà.   In   I_talia   sei cento e quaranta,
Laudes, al_le sind ihm ei_ner_lei, al_le   sind ihm ei_ner_lei.   In   I_talien   sechshundert und vierzig,

in   Alma _ gna   duecento e trent'u _ na.   cen _   to in Francia, in Turchia   no _ cant'una, ma, ma, ma in I_
hier   in Deutschland   zweihundert und neune.   da   in Frankreich nur hun _ dert   und eine, doch, doch, doch, doch in

spagna, ma in I _ spagna, son già mil_le e tre, mille e tre, mille e tre, l'han fra que_ste conta_
Spanien, doch in Spanien sind schon tausenddrei, tausenddrei, tausenddrei. Da sind schmucke Kammer_

di_ ne, ca_me_rie_re, ci_ta _ di _ ne, v'han contes_se, ba_ro _ nes_se, marche_sa_ne, prin_ci _ pesse, e v'han don_ne d'ogni
kätzchen, und hier net_te Bürger_schätzchen, die_se Anzahl Ba_ro _ nes_sen, Ehren_damen und Com_tessen, je_den Standes, jeden

grado, d'ogni forma, d'ogni età, d'o — gni for — ma, d'o — gnie — tà, d'o — gni
Landes, alle sind ihm einer_lei, al — le sind ihm ei — ner — lei, al — le

for — — ma, d'ogni e_tà. Nel_la bionda e_gli ha lu_sanza di lo_dar la genti_lez_za,
sind ihm ei_ner_lei. An der Blonden hör' ich ihn preisen ed_len Geist und holde An_muth,

nel _ la   bruna   la costanza, nel _ la   bian _ ca   la _____ dol _ cezza;   ruol d'in_
an der   Braunen   fe _ ste Treue, an der   Weissen   sanf _ tes Schmachten;   vol _ le

ver _ _ no la grassot _ ta, vuol d'e _ sta _ te la ma grotta;   è la grande   ma e_
sucht   er für den Win _ ter, für den Som _ mer schlanke Kinder;   Gro _ sse nennt er   ma je_

sto_sa,   è la gran___de   ma_e__sto_____sa; la pic-
stätisch,   Gro_sse nennt   er   ma__je__stä_____tisch;und die

ci_na,   la pic_cina,   la pic_cina, la pic_cina, la pic_cina, la pic_cina, la pic_cina, la pic_cina è o_gnor vez-
Kleine,   ja die Kleine,   ja die Kleine,ja die Kleine,ja die Kleine, ja die Kleine, ja die Kleine,ja die Kleine verschmäht er

zo_sa, è o.gnor vezzo_sa,è o.gnor vez_zo_sa. Del _ le vecchie fa___con.qui.sta pel pia _ cer_ di porle in
nimmer,verschmäht er nimmer,verschmäht er nimmer.Auch der Alten nicht___vergisst er, nur zum Scherz für sein Re_

li _ sta; sua passion pre.do_mi_nan _ te_____ è la giovin princi.piante; non si
gi _ ster; stets am meisten er er_glüh _ te_____ für die nur erst Aufge_blühte, niemals

por_ti la gonnel_la, voi sa_pe_te quel che fa, voi sa_pe_te, voi sa_pe_te quel che fa,_____ quel che
Mädchen, sieht er Frauen. Sie er_fuhren wie's da geht, Sie er_fuh_ren, Sie er_fuhren wie's da geht,_____ wie's da

fa,_____ quel che fa,_____ voi sa_pe _ te quel che fa. *(parte.)*
geht,_____ wie's da geht,_____ Sie er_fuh _ ren wie's da geht. *(geht ab.)*

RECITATIVE (ANNA, OTTAVIO) AND ARIA (ANNA), "OR SAI CHI L'ONORE"

This is the big scene in which Anna announces to her fiancé Ottavio that she has recognized the Don as her seducer (he was masked during their encounter), describes the sequence of events, and finally exhorts him to help her take revenge. Here the atmosphere is fully that of the *opera seria:* the recitative is of the elaborate *accompagnato* type, where passages featuring strongly accentuated and dissonant chords alternate with the sustained and subdued accompaniment for most of her narrative. There follows the outstanding revenge aria (bb. 70 ff.—No. 10 in the opera); it is in D major, a key not only usual with such arias but one also associated with the Don and generally with comic opera (see above). Typical are the wide leaps and, later, the coloratura in the vocal part, as well as the active, agitated accompaniment, with its rising figure in the bass and tremolo in the strings; all this may also be associated with the expression of the demonic.[1] The aria is in three-part form with some modifications. The middle part is at b. 86; the restatement of the opening, after a bar in recitative style, is at b. 100; there is also an extended coda (bb. 125 ff.).

Text and translation

RECITATIVE

ANNA:
Don Ottavio, son morta!   Don Ottavio, I'm dead!

OTTAVIO:
Cos'è stato?   What has happened?

ANNA:
Per pietà, soccorretemi!   For pity's sake, help me!

OTTAVIO:
Mio bene, fate coraggio!   My precious, take heart!

ANNA:
O Dei! O Dei!   Oh ye gods! Oh ye gods!
Quegli è il carnefice del padre mio!   That man is my father's murderer!

OTTAVIO:
Che dite?   What are you saying?

ANNA:
Non dubitate piu! Gli ultimi accenti   Doubt no more! The last words
che l'empio proferi, tutta la voce   The villain uttered, his whole voice
richiamar nel cor mio di quell'indegno   Recalled to my heart that worthless
che nel mio apartamento . . .   Creature who, in my apartment . . .

---

[1] Compare this with the principal theme in the first movement of the popular Piano Concerto No. 20 in D Minor (K. 466).

OTTAVIO:
Oh ciel! possible che sotto
il sacro manto d'amicizia . . .
Ma come fu? Narratemi
lo strano avvenimento.

Oh heaven! Is't possible that beneath
The sacred cloak of friendship . . .
But how was it? Tell me about
The strange happening.

ANNA:
Era già alquanto avanzata la notte

quando nelle mie stanze, ove soletta

mi trovai per sventura, entrar io vidi,

in un mantello avvolto,
un uom che al primo istante
avea preso per voi,
ma riconobbi poi
che un inganno era il mio!

The night was already somewhat
advanced
When into my apartments, where
alone
I found myself by mischance, I saw
enter,
Wrapped in a cloak,
A man, who at the first instant
I took for you,
But I realized afterwards
That I had been deceived!

OTTAVIO:
Stelle! seguite.

Heavens! Go on.

ANNA:
Tacito a me s'appressa
e mi vuole abbracciar:
scioglermi cerco
ei più mi stringe; io grido!
Non viene alcun; con una mano
cerca d'impedire la voce,
e coll'altra m'afferra stretta
così che già mi credo vinta.

Silent, he approaches me
And would embrace me:
I seek to free myself;
He presses me more tightly; I cry out!
No one comes; with one hand
He seeks to stop my mouth,
And with the other holds me tight,
So that I think myself already
overcome.

OTTAVIO:
Perfido! E alfin?

Perfidious wretch! And finally?

ANNA:
Alfine il duol, l'orrore
dell'infame attentato
accrebbe sì la lena mia,
che a forza di svincolarmi,

torcermi e piegarmi,
da lui mi sciolsi.

Finally, the pain, the horror
Of the infamous attempt
So increased my strength
That by force of wrenching myself
free,
Twisting and bending,
I broke away from him.

OTTAVIO:
Ohimè! Respiro!

Oh goodness! I breathe again!

ANNA:
Allora rinforzo i stridi miei,
chiamo soccorso; fugge il fellon;

Then I increase my cries,
I call for help; the villain flees;

arditamente il seguo fin nella strada	Boldly I follow him into the street
per fermarlo, e sono	To stop him, and am myself
assalatrice ed assalita!	Both assailant and assailed!
Il padre v'accorre, vuol	My father comes running thither,
conoscerlo,	would know who he is,
e l'indegno, che del povero vecchio	And the vile wretch who was stronger
era più forte,	than the old man,
compiè il misfatto suo col dargli	Completed his crime by killing him.
morte.	

ARIA

Or sai chi l'onore	Now you know who would have torn
Rapire a me volse,	My honor from me,
Che fu il traditore	Who was the traitor
Che il padre mi tolse.	Who deprived me of my father.
Vendetta ti chieggo,	I ask you for vengeance,
La chiede il tuo cor.	Your heart demands it too.
Rammenta la piaga	Remember the wound
Del misero seno,	In that unhappy breast,
Rimira di sangue	See once more the ground
Coperto il terreno,	Soaked in blood,
Se l'ira in te langue	If in you should languish
D'un giusto furor.	The fury of a just indignation.
Or sai chi l'onore, *etc.*	Now you know, who would have
	torn, *etc.*
Rammenta la piaga,	Remember the wound,
Rimira di sangue,	See once more the blood,
Vendetta ti chieggo,	I ask you for vengeance,
La chiede il tuo cor.	Your heart demands it too.

Recitative (*Anna, Ottavio*) and Aria (*Anna*), "Or sai chi l'onore"

ne_fi_ce del padre mi_o.   Non du_bi_ta_te più:gli ultimi accenti   che l'empio pro_fe_rì,   tut_ta, la
tödte_te den theuren Va_ter.   Zweifeln darfst du nicht mehr! die letztenWorte,   die   er zum Abschied sprach,Ton,Blick und

Che di_te!
Was hör'ich!

vo_ce   richiamar nel cor mio di quell'in_degno che nel mio apparta_mento...
Stimme, al_les liess den Verworfnen mich er_kennen,der jüngst in meiner Wohnung...

Oh   ciel!   pos_si_bi_le che sotto il sa_cro
O   Gott!   wär's möglich wohl,dass unter heil'ger

Andante.

E_ra già alquanto   a_van
Schon war der   Abend dunkelnd

man_to   d'a_mi_ci_zia...Ma co_me fu,   narrate_mi, lo strano avveni_men_to.
Freundschaft trautem Schleier... Doch was geschah? erzähle mir den grauenvollen Hergang.

za_ta la not_te, quando nel_le mie stanze, o _ ve so_let_ta mi tro_vai per sven _ tu_ra, en_trar io vi_di in un mantello av-
nie_der_gesunken, als in mei_ne Ge_mächer, wo ich zu meinem Unglück völlig al _ lein war, ein Mann hereintritt, verhüllt in ei_nen

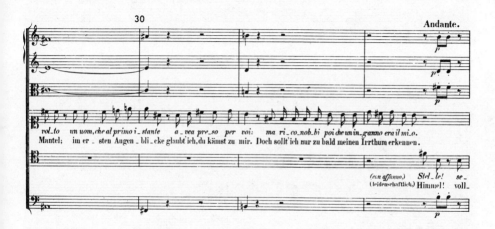

30

Andante.

rol_to un uom, che al primo i_stante a _ vea pre_so per voi: ma ri_co_nob_bi poi che un in_ganno era il mi_o.
Mantel; im er _ sten Augen_bli_cke glaubt'ich, du kämst zu mir. Doch sollt'ich nur zu bald meinen Irrthum erkennen.

(con affanno.) Stel _ le! se _
(leidenschaftlich.) Himmel! voll_

stringendo il tempo

Ta_ci _ to a me s'ap_pressa e mi vuol abbracciar; scio gliermi cerco, ei più mi stringe; io grido,
Schweigend schleicht er mir näher, schlingt um mich seinen Arm; ich widerstre_be, er hält mich fester, ich ru_fe.

gui_te!
en _ de!

so_no   as_sa_li_tri_ce d'as_sa _ li_ta!   Il pa_dre v'ac_cor_re,   vuol co_no_scerlo,   e l'in_
führt'ich   herbei den unglücksel'gen Zweikampf!   Mein Va_ter will hel_fen,   will er_kennen ihn; doch der

degno, che del po_ve_ro recchio e _ ra più for_te,   compie il misfat_to suo,   compie il misfatto su_o   col dargli morte.
Frevler_ ü_berle_gen an Kräften dem schwachen Greise   häuft sei_ne Missethaten,   häuft sei_ne Missethaten, raubt ihm das Leben.

per _ to, co_per_ toil ter _ re_no, se li_rain te langue d'un giu _ sto fu _ ror,   d'un giusto fu_ ror,   Or
tränk_te, es tränk _ te den Boden, dies feu_re aufs neu_e zur Ra _ che dich an,   zur Rache dich an!   Du

sai chi l'ò _ no_re   ra _ pi _ re a me volse,   chi fu il tra _ di _ to_re che il padre, che il pa_dre mi
kennst den Ver _ räther,   der Schan _ de mir drohte,   mit mör _ dri _ schem Stahle den Vater, den Va_ter mir

tol _ se: ven _ det _ ta ti ___ chieggio,   la   chie _ de il tuo ___ cor, _____   la __
raub _ te: zur   Ra _ che ruft   Eh _ re,   ent _ flammt dich dein   Herz, _____   ent _

chie _ de il tuo cor.   Rammen _ ta   la piaga,   ri _ mi _ ra   il sangue. Ven _ det _ ta, ti __ chieggio,   la
flammt dich dein Herz.   Ge _ den _ ke   der Wunde, ge _ den _ ke   des Blutes! Zur   Ra _ che   ruft   Eh _ re,   ent _

chie _ de il tuo cor,_____ la___ chie _ de il tuo cor. Ven_det_ta ti chieggio, la chie_ de il tuo
flammt dich dein Herz,_____ ent _ flammt dich dein Herz. Zur Rache ruft Eh _ re, entflammt dich dein

cor, ven_det_ta ti chieggio, la chie_ de il tuo cor, la chie _ de il tuo cor, la chie _ de il tuo
Herz, zur Rache ruft Eh _ re, entflammt dich dein Herz, entflammt dich __ dein Herz, entflammt _ dich dein Herz, ent _ flammt dich dein

cor,   la chie_de il tuo cor;   ven_detta ti chieggio, la chiede il tuo cor. (parte.)

Herz,   ent_flammt dich dein Herz, zur Rache, zur Rache entflammt dich dein Herz. (geht ab.)

EXCERPT ("MINUET" SCENE), FROM FINALE, ACT I

This represents perhaps the most extraordinary exploitation of the eighteenth-century convention regarding the operatic finale (see above, p. 396); the increase in action is linked to the suspense associated with the Don's attempted seduction of Zerlina, all ingeniously presented with the unparalleled use of on-stage orchestras. The three parts of the excerpt are as follows:

First: A march-like Maestoso in C major, as Leporello welcomes the masked guests (Anna, Elvira, and Ottavio; but he does not yet know their identity) and all join in a pompous toast to freedom ("Viva la libertà").

Second: The main orchestra strikes up a minuet (b. 47) in G major and all begin to dance, the Don with Zerlina. In succession two on-stage orchestras begin to tune (which tuning Mozart writes out) and play first a contredanse (country dance) and then a fast waltz respectively. The simultaneous performance of the three dances creates a complex jumble of rhythms and sounds (with a distinctly twentieth-century flavor about it—in principle, at least) against which the Don presses his advances. This accumulation of sound and tension is suddenly broken and resolved by Zerlina's scream, leading immediately to—

Third: Anna, Elvira, and Ottavio move to the rescue (b. 109), as Masetto first commiserates with Zerlina's plight and then joins them; they advance together against the Don and Leporello. The harmonies here move from G major through E-flat major, B-flat minor, and C minor, ending in D minor.

Text and translation

LEPORELLO:
Venite pur avanti,
vezzose mascherette.

Come forward then,
Charming little maskers.

GIOVANNI:
È aperto a tutti quanti.
Viva la libertà!

It's open to all and sundry.
Hurrah for liberty!

TUTTI:
Viva la libertà!

Hurrah for liberty!

ANNA, ELVIRA, AND OTTAVIO:
Siam grati a tanti segni
di generosità.

We are grateful for so many marks
Of generosity.

GIOVANNI:
Ricominciate il suono.
Tu accoppia i ballerini.

Strike up the music again.
You pair off the dancers.

LEPORELLO:
Da bravi, via, ballate.

Come on, then, dance away.

ELVIRA:
Quella è la contadina.   That is the peasant girl.

ANNA:
Io moro!   I'm dying!

OTTAVIO:
Simulate.   Dissemble.

LEPORELLO AND MASETTO:
Va bene, in verità!   Going fine? Everything's going fine!

GIOVANNI:
A bada tien Masetto.   Beware, keep Masetto occupied.
Il tuo compagno io sono.   I am your partner,
Zerlina, vien pur qua . . .   Zerlina, come here then . . .

LEPORELLO:
Non balli, poveretto?   Aren't you dancing, poor thing? poor
                                                    thing?
Vien qua, Masetto caro,   Come here, Masetto, my dear fellow!
facciam quel ch'altri fa.   Let's join the others.

MASETTO:
No, no, ballar non voglio.   No, no, I don't want to dance.

LEPORELLO:
Eh! balla, amico mio.   Come on, dance, my friend.

ANNA:
Resister non poss'io!   Hold out I cannot!

ELVIRA AND OTTAVIO:
Fingete, per pietà.   Pretend, for pity's sake.

GIOVANNI:
Vieni con me, mia vita . . .   Come with me, my life . . .

ZERLINA:
Oh Numi! son tradita! . . .   O heavens! I am betrayed!

MASETTO:
Lasciami . . . Ah . . . no . . .   Leave me alone! . . . Ah . . . No
   Zerlina?   . . . Zerlina?

LEPORELLO:
(aside)
Qui nasce una ruina.   Some mischief is afoot here!

ANNA, ELVIRA, AND OTTAVIO:
L'iniquo da se stesso nel laccio   The wretch is walking into the trap of
   se ne va.   his own accord.

ZERLINA:
Gente! . . . aiuto! . . . aiuto! gente!

Good people! . . . help! . . . help! good people!

ANNA, ELVIRA, AND OTTAVIO:
Soccorriamo l'innocente . . .

Let's save the innocent . . .

MASETTO:
Ah! Zerlina! . . .

Oh! Zerlina!

ZERLINA:
Scellerato!

Villain!

ANNA, ELVIRA, AND OTTAVIO:

Ora grida da quel lato . . .
Ah! getiamo giù la porta . . .

Now, she's calling from that side . . .
Oh! let's push the door down . . .

ZERLINA:
Soccorretemi, o son morta! . . .

Save me, oh, save me! I am dead!

ANNA, ELVIRA, OTTAVIO, AND
   MASSETTO:
Siam qui noi per tua difesa.

We are here to defend you.

Excerpt, "Minuet Scene" from Finale, Act I

Siam grati a tan_ti se _ gni di ge_ne_ro_si_ tà, di ge _ ne _ ro_si_
Wir danken Ih_rer Gü _ te, wir schätzen freien Sinn, wir schä_tzen frei_en

Siam grati a tan_ti se _ gni di ge_ne_ro_si_ tà, di ge _ ne _ ro_si_
Wir danken Ih_rer Gü _ te, wir schätzen freien Sinn, wir schä_tzen frei_en

Siam grati a tan_ti se _ gni di ge_ne_ro_si_ tà, di ge _ ne _ ro_si_
Wir danken Ih_rer Gü _ te, wir schätzen freien Sinn, wir schä_tzen frei_en

perto a tut_ti quanti, ri_va la li_ber _ tà!
kommen sind hier Al_le, hier lebt ein freier Sinn!

Trio (Elvira, Don Giovanni, Leporello), "Ah! taci, ingiusto core"

This selection well illustrates Mozart's way with the ensemble, a most important element in *opera buffa*. In this scene the Don and Leporello have exchanged cloaks, and the Don sings a serenade to Elvira on the balcony, but in such a way that Leporello (disguised as the Don) appears to be doing the singing. The key is A major, which in the opera is associated with amorous persuasion. The trio is in a three-part scheme related to the sonata structure (here, with an episode replacing the development) and thus to the Da Capo aria. It may be outlined as follows:

	Bar	
Exposition	1	*Principal key and theme:* Elvira's lyrical grieving.
	14	Transition: Leporello and the Don comment on the situation, using a new motive.
	19	*Secondary theme:* The Don begins his lyrical persuasion, using Elvira's opening theme; Elvira begins to waver (symbolized by her use of the transition figure previously associated with the Don and Leporello), as Leporello wonders at her.
Episode	35	The Don presses on with a new tune, now in C major, and Elvira gradually gives way, to Leporello's satirical laughter.
Recapitulation	54	*Principal theme.*
(Compressed)	67	Transition.
	74	*Secondary theme* (shortened).
Coda	79	

Text and translation

ELVIRA:
Ah! taci, ingiusto core,
Non palpitarmi in seno;
È un empio, è un traditore,
È colpa aver pietà.

Oh! Be silent, unfair heart;
Do not beat so in my breast;
He is a wicked fellow, a traitor,
'Tis a sin to feel sorry for him.

LEPORELLO:
(*sottovoce*)
Zitto . . . di Donna Elvira,
Signor, la voce io sento.

Sh . . . I hear Donna Elvira's
voice, sir.

GIOVANNI:
(*sottovoce*)
Cogliere io vo' il momento.

I would take advantage of the
opportunity;

Tu fermati un po' là.	You stand there a little.
Elvira, idolo mio!	Elvira, my adored!

ELVIRA:
Non è costui l'ingrato?	Is not that fellow the ungrateful wretch?

GIOVANNI:
Sì, vita, mia, son io,	Yes, my life, it is I
E chiedo carità.	And I ask forgiveness.

ELVIRA:
(aside)
Numi, che strano affetto	Gods, what a strange feeling
Mi si risveglia in petto!	Is stirring in my breast.

LEPORELLO:
(aside)
State a veder la pazza,	You'll see the mad girl
Che ancor gli crederà!	Will believe in him again!

GIOVANNI:
Discendi, o gioia bella!	Come down, o lovely jewel!
Vedrai che tu sei quella	You will see that you're the one
Che adora l'alma mia:	My soul adores!
Pentito io sono già.	I've repented already.

ELVIRA:
No, non ti credo, o barbaro.	No, I don't believe you, o cruel man!

GIOVANNI:
Ah, credimi, o m'uccido.	Oh! Believe me, or I shall kill myself!

LEPORELLO:
(*sottovoce*)
Se seguitate, io rido.	If you keep on, I shall laugh.

GIOVANNI:
Idolo mio, vien qua.	My idol, come here.

ELVIRA:
(aside)
Dei, che cimento è questo!	O Gods, what a hazard is this!
Non so s'io vado o resto . . .	I don't know whether to go or stay.
Ah! proteggete voi	Oh, protect, ye gods
La mia credulità.	My credulity.

GIOVANNI:
(aside)
Spero che cada presto;	I think she'll fall soon.
Che bel colpetto è questo!	What a fine stroke is this!
Più fertile talento	A talent more prolific than mine
Del mio, no, non si dà.	There is not.

LEPORELLO:
(aside)
Già quel mendace labbro   Those false lips
Torna a sedur costei;   Are already seducing this girl again;
Deh, proteggete, o Dei,   Protect, o gods,
La sua credulità.   Her credulity.

Trio (*Elvira, Don Giovanni, Leporello*), "Ah! taci, ingiusto core"

Cogliere io vo'il momen_to; tu fermatiun pò là! tu fermatiun pò là! (si mette dietro Lep.) El_
Das ist mir sehr willkommen, nimm meine Stelle ein, nimm meine Stelle ein. (stellt sich hinter Lep.) El_

vi_ra, Si_gnor, la voce io sen_to.
Stimme, wohl hab'ich sie vernommen.

Non è costui l'in_
Ich höre den Ver_

vi_ra, ido_lo mio!
vi_ra, du Geliebte!

El_vi_ra, ido_lo mi_o...
El_vi_ra, du Ge_liebte...

gio — ja bel — la, ve — drai che tu sei quel — la che a do — ra l'al — ma mi — a: pen

komm' du En — gel, dass ich dir Zeugniss ge — be, wie dir allein ich le — be; sieh

No, non ti cre — do, o bar — ba — ro, no, non ti cre — do, o bar — ba — ro,

Nein, nimmer kann ich glauben dir, nein, nimmer kann ich glau — ben dir,

ti — to io so — no già! Ah, cre — di — mi, ah,

mich vol — ler Reu — e nah'n. O glaube mir, o

questo?
Bangen:

presto!
langen:

labbro
fangen,

Non so s'io vado,o resto?
hör'ich auf sein Verlangen?

Che bel colpet_to e questo!
süss meine Worte klangen.

torna a se_dur co_ste_i!
sie ist ins Netzgegangen.

Ah,pro _ _ teg_ge_te _
Beschü _ _ tze mich,o

Più fer_ti_le ta_len_to
Wie ich die Kunst verste_he,

Deh,pro _ _ teg_ge_te,
Beschü _ _ tze sie, güt'

del mio, no,non si
verstcht sie Nie_maud

oh
_ _ ger

vo_i
Himmel,

dà, più fer_ti_le ta_lento,
mehr,wie ich die Kunst ver_stehe,

Dei,
Himmel,

la mia cre_du_li_tà, cre_du_li_tà!
ver _ trau'ich ihm,vertrau'ich ihm zu sehr.

no,del mio,no, non si _ dà.
nein,versteht sie Niemand mehr.

la sua cre_du_li_tà, cre_du_li_tà.
sie traut ihm viel zu sehr,ihm viel zu sehr.

Dei! che ci _ mento è questo?
Ich fühl'ein seltsam Bangen,

Spe_ro che 'ca_da
Ich werd' an's Ziel ge_

Dei! che ci _ mento è
hör' ich auf sein Ver_

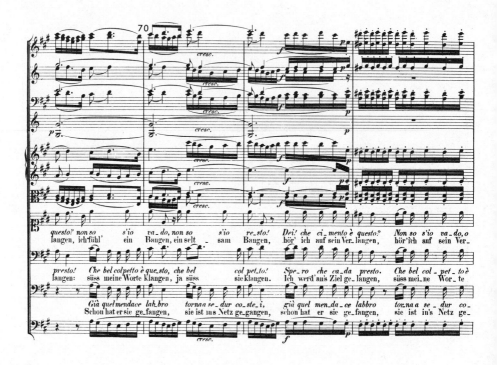

tà; cre _ du _ li _ tà, la mia __ cre _ du _ li _ tà, la mia cre _ du _ li _ tà. *(parte dal balcone.)*
trau' ich ihm zu sehr, ver_trau'__ ich ihm zu sehr, ver_trau' ich ihm zu sehr. *(sie geht vom Balkon.)*

mio, no, non vi dà. no, non si dà. no, non si dà.
steht sie Niemand mehr. nein, Niemand mehr, nein, Niemand mehr.

ta, cre _ du _ li _ tà, cre _ du _ li _ tà, cre _ du _ li _ tà.
sehr, ihm viel zu sehr, ihm viel zu sehr, ihm viel zu sehr.

Aria (Ottavio), "Il mio tesoro"

This aria, in the *opera seria* style, provides a good characterization of Don Ottavio, whose noble status is confirmed by the use of B-flat major, in the three-part form (related to the Da Capo structure), with military fanfares and coloratura in the middle section. Here is Mozart's lyrical cantilena at its best. The outline is: principal section—middle or secondary section (bb. 29 ff.)—return of the principal section (bb. 49 ff.)—coda (bb. 70 ff.), using elements from the middle section.

Text and translation

Il mio tesoro intanto	Go to my treasure meanwhile
Andate a consolar,	And console her,
E del bel ciglio il pianto	And from her lovely eyes
Cercate di asciugar.	Seek to wipe away the tears.
Ditele, che i suoi torti	Tell her her wrongs
A vendicar io vado,	I go to avenge,
Che sol di stragi e morti	That only as messenger of carnage and death
Nunzio vogl'io tornar.	Will I return.
Il mio tesoro intanto, *etc.*	Go to my treasure meanwhile, *etc.*

Aria (*Ottavio*), "Il mio tesoro"

23. Selections from *Die Zauberflöte* ["The Magic Flute" K. 620]: Song, "Der Vogelfänger bin ich ja"; Song, "O Isis und Osiris"; Excerpt, from Finale, Act II

In September 1791 Mozart, in collaboration with the impressario and actor Emanuel Schikaneder, produced this extraordinary work. Apparently the original intent was to have a "Turkish" musical play (*Singspiel*) featuring a rescue, which would thus be much like the earlier *Die Entführung aus dem Serail* (see p. 394 above), but with the element of magic added: Prince Tamino is to rescue Pamina, daughter of the Queen of the Night, from the evil magician Sarastro, with the assistance of Papageno, the bird-man, and the protection of the powerful Magic Flute. Somehow and somewhere a change in direction was made, so that the Queen of the Night turns out to be evil, while Sarastro becomes the incarnation of virtue (the proper association is with the sun-god Zoroaster). So the plot swings, with Tamino and Pamino finally both joining Sarastro and having to prove themselves worthy by passing a series of ordeals. Thus in scope the work is much larger than the usual *Singspiel*.

In this change of emphasis freemasonry played an important role. The printed vocal score is decorated with masonic symbols: the five-pointed star, the hourglass, the square and trowel. Moralizing sentiments appear over and over in the text. The symbolism of the number three is important: there are three ladies who accompany the Queen of the Night, three boys who guide Tamino on his quest, three ceremonial chords on the brass and wind instruments, and three flats in the key signature (E-flat major). The distinctive instrumentation in some of the numbers is the same as that Mozart used in pieces composed specifically for the masons.

As in *Don Giovanni*, musical types and styles are used for characterization. The Queen of the Night sings elaborate arias and accompanied recitatives,[1] with coloratura of the most difficult kind; Tamino and Pamina also from time to time use forms of the Italian *opera seria*. Sarastro, on the other hand, embodying the highest virtue, uses solemn and dignified German song types, in strophic form. Papageno has comic songs, also in strophic form. Other characters move in between. Thus the work encompasses a great variety of musical styles and expressive qualities.

The three examples selected here show some of this range. The first, Papageno's song, "Der Vogelfänger bin ich ja" (No. 2 of the work), in which he introduces himself, is a simple strophic and comic number which in principle would not be out of place in an ordinary *Singspiel*[2]; the figure in the piccolo helps with the comedy. The second brings us to the masonic aspect, a serious song for Sarastro with chorus, "O Isis und Osiris" (No. 10). Its measured melodic line emphasizes the bass register; its male chorus and an extraordinary wind ensemble with basset horns (alto clarinets) and trombones are typical of Mozart's masonic pieces. Structurally the song is strophic, but the music changes for the first part of the second strophe.

The third example, in some ways the most extraordinary, comes from the finale of Act II, as Tamino and Pamina prepare for the final ordeal—walking through fire and water. After a sombre, adagio ceremonial opening we are presented with a contrapuntal piece which is a setting of a German hymn (usually sung to the words, "O Gott vom Himmel sieh darein"); here it is sung by the two armed men, in long note-values accompanied by a fugue in the orchestra. In principle this passage is like a chorale-prelude or the first movement of a cantata by Bach. Thus, to characterize the seriousness of the situation Mozart falls back on older techniques specifically associated with religious music. Thereafter the character of the scene changes quickly, with Tamino's short arioso and the allegretto quartet for Pamina, Tamino and the armed men.

Texts and translations

SONG FOR PAPAGENO

Der Vogelfänger bin ich ja,	A merry birdcatcher am I,
Stets lustig, heissa, hopsassa!	Aye merrily tra-la I cry;
Ich Vogelfänger bin bekannt	As birdcatcher it is my pride
Bei alt und jung im ganzen Land.	That I'm renowned on every side.
Weiss mit dem Locken umzugehn	To lure the birds it is my art;
Und mich aufs Pfeifen zu verstehn.	My piping tune they know by heart.
Drum kann ich froh und lustig sein,	So may I glad and merry be,
Denn alle Vögel sind ja mein.	For all my birds belong to me.

[1] For an impressive sample of the accompanied recitative, see Godwin, *Schirmer Scores*, No. 34, pp. 254–63.

[2] For other instances of this type, see *ibid.*, pp. 252–4 and 264–6.

Der Vogelfänger bin ich ja,
Stets lustig, heissa, hopsassa!
Ich Vogelfänger bin bekannt
Bei alt und jung im ganzen Land.
Ein Netz für Mädchen möchte ich,
Ich fing sie dutzendweis für mich!
Dann sperrte ich sie mir ein,
Und alle Mädchen wären mein.

A merry birdcatcher am I,
Aye merrily tra-la I cry;
As birdcatcher it is my pride
That I'm renowned on every side.
And yet I'd love to catch a maid,
A score would in my snare be laid;
I'd mew her up and make her fast,
And then they'd all be mine at last.

Wenn alle Mädchen wären mein,
So tauschte ich brav Zucker ein:
Die, welche mir am liebsten wär,
Der gäb ich gleich den Zucker her.
Und küsste sie mich zärtlich dann,
Wär sie mein Weib und ich ihr Mann.
Sie schlief an meiner Seite ein,
Ich wiegte wie ein Kind sie ein.

And when they all were mine at last,
Some sugar barter for repast,
And give to her who was most dear
A sugar loaf to bring her cheer.
And then she'd kiss me tenderly
And so we man and wife would be.
So soft in sleep by me she'd lie,
While I to her sang lullaby.

Song for Sarastro

SARASTRO:
O, Isis und Osiris, schenket
Der Weisheit Geist dem neuen Paar!

Bestow, O Isis and Osiris
On this young pair your wisdom's
power!

Die ihr den Schritt der Wand'rer
lenket,
Stärkt mit Geduld sie in Gefahr.

Ye who direct the wanderers' feet,
give
Patience and strength in danger's hour.

CHORUS:
Stärkt mit Geduld sie in Gefahr.

Patience and strength in danger's hour.

SARASTRO:
Lasst sie der Prüfung Früchte sehen;
Doch sollten sie zu Grabe gehen,

Grant them reward of all their trial;
Yet should they fall in Death's dark
snare,

So lohnt der Tugend kühnen Lauf,
Nehmt sie in euren Wohnsitz auf.

Honor their virtue's high assayal,
Them to thy resting place repair.

CHORUS:
Nehmt sie in euren Wohnsitz auf.

Them to thy resting place repair.

Excerpt, from Finale, Act II

Two great mountains. One throwing
water, other spitting fire.
Tamino. Two men in black armor.

The Armed Men

Der, welcher wandert diese Strasse
voll Beschwerden,
Wird rein durch Feuer, Wasser, Luft
und Erden;

He who shall tread this path so full of
trial
Fire, water, air and earth shall un-
defile.

Wenn er des Todes Schrecken über-
winden kann,
Schwingt er sich der Erde himmelan.

And when he shall have conquered
death's fear
Then shall he rise from earth to
heaven's sphere.

Erleuchtet wird er dann imstande sein,
Sich den Mysterien der Isis ganz zu
weihn.

Illumined shall he be, and consecrate,
All to the mysteries of Isis dedicate.

TAMINO
Mich schreckt kein Tod, als Mann zu
handeln,
Den Weg der Tugend fortzuwandeln.
Schliesst mir die Schreckenspforten
auf,
Ich wage froh den kühnen Lauf.
(*turns to depart*)

I fear not death, but like a man

Tread virtue's path that I began.
If on me terror's gate shall ope

I shall dare all, yet live in hope.

PAMINA
(*from within*)
Tamino, halt! Ich muss dich sehn.

Tamino, stay! I must thee see.

TAMINO
Was hör ich? Paminens Stimme?

What do I hear? That voice? Pamina!

THE ARMED MEN
Ja, ja, das ist Paminens Stimme.

Ay, sure that is Pamina calling.

TAMINO
Wohl mir, nun kann sie mit mir gehn,
Nun trennet uns kein Schicksal mehr,
Wenn auch der Tod beschieden wär!

Ah, joy! now she may go with me.
No destiny doth sunder us
Even if we be doomed to die.

THE ARMED MEN
Wohl dir, nun kann sie mit dir gehn,
Nun trennet euch kein Schicksal mehr,
Wenn auch der Tod beschieden wär!

Ah, joy! Now she may go with thee.
No destiny can sunder ye,
Even if ye be doomed to die.

TAMINO
Ist mir erlaubt, mit ihr zu sprechen?

Is't granted I may speak with her?

THE ARMED MEN
Dir ist erlaubt, mit ihr zu sprechen!

'Tis granted; thou may'st speak with
her.

TAMINO
Welch Glück, wenn wir uns wieder-
sehn,

What joy if we may meet again!

THE ARMED MEN
Welch Glück, wenn wir euch wieder-
sehn.

What joy, if we meet ye again.

Tamino, The Armed Men

Froh Hand in Hand in Tempel gehn.   Toward the temple, hand in hand.
Ein Weib, das Nacht und Tod nicht   A maid that shuns nor death nor night
    scheut,
Ist würdig und wird eingeweiht.   Is worthy to be consecrate.

(Pamina is led in by the second Priest.)

Pamina

Tamino mein! O welch ein Glück!   O my Tamino! O what joy!

Tamino

Pamina mein, o welch ein Glück!   O my Pamina, O what joy!
Hier sind die Schreckenspforten,   Here stand the gates of terror,
Die Not und Tod mir dräun.   Where death and darkness loom.

Pamina

Ich werde aller Orten   I shall be, come what may now
An deiner Seite sein,   Be ever at thy side;
Ich selber führe dich,   Myself shall lead thee on
Die Liebe leitet mich.   As love my guide shall be.
Sie mag den Weg mit Rosen streun,   We'll find our path with roses strewn,
Weil Rosen stets bei Dornen sein.   For roses e'er in thorns do bloom.
Spiel du die Zauberflöte an,   Play thou upon thy magic flute,
Sie schütze uns auf unsrer Bahn.   It shall us on our way protect.
Es schnitt in einer Zauberstunde   'Twas carved in a magic hour
Mein Vater sie aus tiefstem Grunde   By my dear father, from the deepest
Der tausendjähr'gen Eiche aus,   Of the thousand-year-old oak,
Bei Blitz und Donner, Sturm und   In lightning, thunder, tempest, storm.
    Braus.
Nun komm und spiel die Flöte an,   Now come, do thou on thy flute play;
Sie leite uns auf grauser Bahn.   It shall us cheer on terror's way.

Pamina, Tamino

Wir wandeln durch des Tones Macht,   We tread with music as our shield
Froh durch des Todes düstre Nacht!   Through murky death's own darkest
                                             field!

The Armed Men

Ihr wandelt durch des Tones Macht,   Ye tread with music as our shield
Froh durch des Todes düstre Nacht.   Through murky death's own darkest
                                             field!

Song (*Papageno*), "Der Vogelfänger bin ich ja"

1. Der Vo _ gel _ fän _ ger bin ich ja, stets lu _ stig, hei _ ssa! hop _ sa _ sa! ich Vo _ gel _ fän _ ger
2. Der Vo _ gel _ fän _ ger bin ich ja, stets lu _ stig, hei _ ssa! hop _ sa _ sa! ich Vo _ gel _ fän _ ger
3. Wenn al _ le Mädchen wä _ ren mein, so tausch _ te ich brav Zu _ cker ein, die wel _ che mir am

bin be _ kannt bei alt und jung im gan _ zen Land.
bin be _ kannt bei alt und jung im gan _ zen Land.
liebsten wär,' der gäb' ich gleich den Zu _ cker her.

Weiss mit dem Lo _ cken
Ein Netz für Mäd _ chen
Und küss _ te sie mich

um _ zu _ gehn, und mich auf's Pfei _ fen zu ver _ stehn.
möchte ich; ich fing sie dut _ zend _ weis für mich.
zärt _ lich dann, wär' sie mein Weib und ich ihr Mann.

Drum kann ich froh und
Dann sperr _ te ich sie
Sie schlief an mei _ ner

lus _ tig sein, denn al _ le Vö _ gel sind ja mein.
bei mir ein, und al _ le Mädchen wä _ ren mein.
Sei _ te ein, ich wieg _ te wie ein Kind sie ein.

Song (*Sarastro, with Chorus*), "O Isis und Osiris"

Excerpt, from Finale, Act II

streu'n, weil Ro_sen stets bei Dor_nen sein. Spiel' du die Zau_ber _ flö _ te an; sie schü_tze

uns auf uns_rer Bahn; es schnitt in ei_ner Zauber_stun_de mein Vater sie aus tief_stem

Grun_de der tau_send jähr'gen Ei_che aus, bei Blitz und Don _ ner, Sturm und Braus. Nun

4

BEETHOVEN

BORN IN BONN IN 1770, Beethoven grew up in the culture of the French Enlightenment. In his early years he developed those ideals of personal and political freedom, human equality and brotherhood, respect for intellectual ability and artistic genius, and belief in the ethical and moral role of the artist in society that he carried with him throughout his life.

In 1792 he moved to Vienna, where he remained for the rest of his life. Here he was able to succeed where barely a decade earlier Mozart had failed: He was able to gain entry to the salons of the aristocracy, he gave successful public performances, began to get his works published, and attracted pupils. He described the situation with respect to publishing clearly enough in an 1801 letter to a friend: "Everything I write now I can immediately sell five times over and get a good price for it—I demand, they pay. You can see it's a pleasant situation." [1]

But this optimism was shattered by impending deafness. Yet, for reasons he made clear in the *Heiligenstadt Testament*, Beethoven continued to compose despite this seemingly insurmountable handicap: His indomitable spirit has been an ideal ever since. In 1808 he negotiated an agreement with three of his aristocratic patrons whereby they agreed to pay him an annual salary, as it were, subject only to the condition that he continue to reside in Vienna —such was his reputation. While he subsequently had difficulties in collecting this, his basic position is clear enough.

His last years were characterized by withdrawal and isolation, and the years immediately after the Congress of Vienna (1814–5) saw a drastic decline in his productivity. Apart from the fact that by 1818 his deafness had become almost total, there were the difficulties involved with the guardianship of his nephew Karl, and the climate of reactionary politics under Prince Metternich. Yet he began to compose once more in earnest after 1819, producing unprecedented works, among them the famous Ninth Symphony. He died in March of 1827.

[1] Paraphrased from the letter to Wegeler, 29 June 1801. See the *Letters of Beethoven,* translated and edited by Emily Anderson I (New York, 1961), p. 58, no. 51.

24.   Sonata No. 7 for Piano in D Major (op. 10 iii)

This work, composed in 1796–8 and published in 1798, thus standing near the beginning of Beethoven's career as a composer, conforms in most respects to eighteenth-century conceptions of the piano sonata: The several movements are contrasting in character but have much variety within each one; traditional keys, key-relationships, and formal schemes exist within the individual movements. Less in keeping with eighteenth-century norms for the piano sonata is the seriousness of the work; it is a large and elaborate affair, with great range of expression. Symbolic of this size and seriousness is the use of the four-movement scheme, previously associated more with string quartets, quintets and symphonies. This last comparison in particular may provide a clue: In its length and elaboration the sonata indeed resembles a symphony. The use of the bright D major here fosters the impression. The sonata has much of these characteristics in common with other early works of Beethoven.

The first movement in particular impresses with its length, brilliance, and variety having a large number of thematic elements, extensive motivic development, great rhythmic drive and vitality, use of changes in dynamics, and much use of figuration.

Of the second-movement Largo in D minor Beethoven, as quoted by Schindler, said that here the listener would sense "the spiritual condition of a person consumed by melancholy" and "the many nuances of light and shadows in this portrait of depression." [1] The instruction at the beginning, *mesto* ("sad"), makes this clear. In the three-part structure, the principal theme in the minor (recurring at b. 44) doubtless represents the "shadow," while the middle part (bb. 30 ff.) represents "light," although one must note the expressive figuration here (bb. 36 ff.) and again in the coda (bb. 72–5), which Beethoven could have derived from C. P. E. Bach and Haydn. This last part,

---

[1] Anton Schindler, *Beethoven as I Knew Him,* translated by C. Jolly, edited by D. MacArdle (Chapel Hill, N.C., 1966), p. 406.

moreover, using elements from both sections of the movement, is a remarkable exploitation of the dynamic and coloristic potentialities of the instrument.

The Minuet is essentially lyrical, with some syncopation and some contrapuntal interest in the part-writing; the Trio, in G major, is simple, and features much crossing of hands.

The finale, a sonata-rondo (first episode at b. 9 and again at b. 64; second episode, a development, at b. 35) is capricious in character—perhaps quasi-improvisational is the right term—with a number of abrupt changes in tempo and dynamics.

Sonata No. 7 for Piano in D Major

Men. D.C, ma senza replica.

RONDO.
Allegro.

25. First Movement from Sonata No. 17 for Piano in D Minor (*The Tempest,* op. 31 ii)

Around 1802 Beethoven began to introduce changes of various kinds into the organization of the multi-movement form of instrumental music. These changes most often took place first in the piano sonatas. Notable examples are seen in the sonatas of op. 26 and 27, in which both the sequence of movements and structural types used in them are different from those in earlier sonatas by Beethoven, as well as most of those by Haydn and Mozart. In the sonatas of op. 27, for instance, a link to another genre is suggested by the title; each is called "sonata quasi una fantasia," thus indicating a certain freedom in formal organization, along with an emphasis on expression and the unexpected.

This trend is continued in the three sonatas of op. 31, published in 1803–4, and is particularly evident in the first movement of the Sonata in D minor reproduced here. The appellation "Tempest," so often applied to this work, comes via Schindler, who, having asked Beethoven to give him an explanation of the work and the later Sonata in F minor (op. 57, "The Appassionata"), received as reply the admonition, "Read Shakespeare's *Tempest*"; a satisfactory explanation of this "explanation" has not as of yet been forthcoming. In any case, the first movement, organized essentially according to the sonata principle, contains a number of elements derived from the fantasia. The principal theme, for one, has improvisational aspects in the slowly arpeggiated opening chord (largo) followed by the furious allegro, staccato figuration, relapsing in an adagio cadence. Its second statement is extended by means of this fast figuration, leading to an assertive second principal theme (bb. 21 ff.), where one notes the contrast between the two elements (bass and treble); this may be related to Schindler's notion of "two principles" alleged to dominate much of Beethoven's music. There is no real relief here at all: certainly not with the secondary theme, rather unusually in the dominant (bb. 41 ff.) nor even later (bb. 55, 63, 69). After the development (bb. 93–142), which works mostly with the second principal theme, the fantasia character returns at the recapitulation: the quasi-improvisational first principal theme is here interrupted by a rhapsodical solo line clearly in the nature of a recitative and doubtless meant to be played in free rhythm (*senza misura*); it is evidently modelled on the fantasias of C. P. E. Bach. Still another improvisational passage (allegro) is interposed (bb. 159–70) before the normal course of the recapitulation is resumed with the secondary theme. There is a brief coda (bb. 221 ff.).

This freedom in the treatment of an established structural type, while certainly present in Haydn, Mozart, and others, becomes much more important in Beethoven.

First Movement from Sonata No. 17 for Piano in D Minor
(*The Tempest*)

26. Symphony No. 3 in E-flat Major
(*Eroica, op. 55*)

As Beethoven continued, his compositions became longer, greater dynamic contrasts were exploited, the use of crescendo and decrescendo became more pronounced, the accents stronger and more intense, the thematic development more concentrated, and the rhythmic element more forceful. Furthermore, many of the new compositions were more clearly associated with Beethoven's ethical ideas concerning the proper role of the artist and of the art-work.

Much of this was manifested at one stroke in what may well be one of the most important musical compositions ever written: the Symphony No. 3 in E-flat Major (op. 55) of 1803–4, first performed in 1805, to which Beethoven himself gave the name *Sinfonia eroica* ("Heroic Symphony"). The story of the intended dedication to Napoleon is well known; in its place Beethoven substituted "to celebrate the memory of a great man." According to a note in the first violin part, Beethoven wished the symphony, because of its great length, to be played toward the beginning of the program rather than toward the end.

Even without the dedication to Napoleon, the association of the work with heroism, with France and the ideals of the French Revolution, which had fired Beethoven's imagination since the early days in Bonn, is clear enough. In connection with the celebration of "the memory of a great man," the second movement is significant: a funeral march for a hero. It had never been usual to include funeral marches in symphonies and similar works, although Beethoven himself already had employed the form in his Sonata for piano in A-flat major (op. 26). It seems that Beethoven was deliberately drawing upon a French custom from the days of the revolution, of mounting large outdoor public funerals for dead military leaders and heroes of the revolution, in which massed brass bands and gigantic choral groups participated. In the finale of the Symphony No. 3 Beethoven brought in another concrete association, this time from Greek mythology: Prometheus, the benefactor of mankind, whom Beethoven had already celebrated in a ballet—and a theme from the ballet is employed in the finale of the symphony.[1]

---

[1] There is some evidence that Beethoven was influenced by Parisian orchestral and operatic music of the 1780s and 1790s by such composers as Cherubini, Méhul, Kreutzer, and

The *Sinfonia eroica* is scored for an orchestra of flutes, oboes, clarinets, bassoons in pairs, three horns, two trumpets, timpani, and strings (an orchestra not much larger than that used in the Symphony No. 1 in C major [op. 21]). It is in four movements, all of which are about double the length they would have had in an eighteenth-century symphony: an opening Allegro in sonata form, the "Marcia funèbre" (Adagio in C minor), the Scherzo and Trio in E-flat major, and the finale, an Allegro, based on the theme from Prometheus.

In the first movement, the heroic character that dominates the work as a whole is immediately established by the two loud E-flat major chords which precede the principal theme. There follows the immediate motivic breaking down of the theme, with sharp accentuations on weak beats, and a dramatic crescendo leading to the fortissimo restatement of the principal theme that ushers in the modulatory passage (bb. 37 ff.). A number of new themes appear here, but particular attention must be directed to the first, a terse motive in dotted rhythm which passes from instrument to instrument and plays an important role as the movement unfolds (bb. 45 ff.). A second crescendo leads to the secondary theme, in B-flat major, first in the winds and then in the strings (bb. 83 ff.). Still another crescendo brings the concluding group, which once more features syncopations and, near the end, *fortissimo* dissonant diminished seventh chords, followed by a brief recalling of the principal theme of the movement.

All the themes appear in the development (bb. 152 ff.), the length of which greatly exceeds that of the exposition (247 bars compared to 151). The principal theme is predominant, appearing both by itself and combined with themes from the modulatory section. Unusual is the introduction of a new theme, in E minor (bb. 284 ff.), one not heard before but which has been regarded as being related to the secondary theme. Finally, some comment has been occasioned by the passage near the end of the development, the so-called re-transition to the recapitulation (bb. 390–98): In a diminuendo, as the strings sound in B-flat harmony, the horn enters softly with the principal theme in E-flat (the tonic) thus making a dissonance. After the recapitulation, which is quite regular, comes a coda, but its length is so great that it has been regarded as a "second development." It, too, uses the new theme that had been introduced in the development. At the very end (bb. 631 ff.) the principal theme is stated four times, each time louder and using more instruments, making a crescendo in stages: first in the horns, then in the first violins, then the lower strings, and then finally, as the trumpets and timpani begin with a "military" triplet figure in the accompaniment, it appears *fortissimo* in the brass instruments, after which the movement rapidly comes to a close.

Grétry; this may be seen in certain of his works as far back as the Symphony in C Major op. 21), where the principal theme of the first movement has been connected with that of Kreutzer's *Overture for the Day Marathon.*

Although it is unusual to have a funeral march in a symphony, there is ample precedent in the *galant* instrumental music of the late eighteenth century for the presence of a march. Since a funeral march is indeed a kind of march, it might be expected to show, to some extent at least, the same formal organization characteristic of a march. In the suites and divertimentos of the time, a march was organized much like a minuet: there would be the march proper, then another march called the trio, after which the march proper is repeated; both march and trio would be disposed according to rounded-binary form. Beethoven's funeral march in the *Sinfonia eroica* plainly has this standard march form in its background, although some important changes have been introduced. The opening portion of the movement, the march proper, displays the rounded-binary form that would be expected, except that double bars are not used, all repetitions being written out in full since the instrumentation is varied. The trio, in C major (bb. 69 ff.), uses triadic and scale figuration as its thematic materials, in the crescendos, martial triplet patterns in the trumpets and timpani are important. Here the rounded-binary form is reduced to a simple ternary scheme with the third part varied (*A B A'*). Now come the departures: After the "bright" trio it seems as if the funeral march is going to be repeated (bb. 104 ff.), but after a few bars there is a sudden interruption and a powerful fugue on a variant in F minor of the funeral march theme is presented (bb. 114 ff.). After the fugue comes to its dramatic end with loud, repeated diminished-seventh chords, the funeral march is again introduced, but in G minor, not C minor, only to be rudely broken off again by a strident fanfare passage employing dotted rhythms in the brass instruments and furious triplets in the strings (bb. 158 ff.). As this subsides, the funeral march is reintroduced, but with the triplet patterns from the fanfare passage retained in the accompaniment (bb. 173 ff.), and this time it continues all the way through. The coda starts at b. 209. At the very end the march theme is heard with simple accompaniment, but broken up with short rests and anxious syncopations which are related to the conventional "sob" figuration pattern of the time and which here have a particularly poignant effect (bb. 238 ff.).

The Scherzo, again in the main key of the work, E-flat major, presents something rather different from the usual minuet: driving rhythms, great crescendos, effective syncopations, and so on. In the trio the use of the three horns as solo instruments with the typical "hunting call" type of thematic material is to be noted.

In the finale, which is based, as we have seen, on a theme from *The Creatures of Prometheus* (1801), we find an unusual type of theme and variations form, one that has some aspects in common with the ostinato form of the Baroque. After an introductory flourish, the bass part of the theme is presented by itself, pizzicato, in the lower strings (bb. 12 ff.); then follow two variations built on this bass part (bb. 44 ff. and bb. 59 ff.), which appear first in the violoncellos and then in the first violins; with the third variation (bb. 75

ff.) the melody proper makes its appearance, first in the oboe, then taken up by the full orchestra. During the rest of the movement the variations, some of which are fugal, draw on either the melody or its bass, or both. Most important are variations IV (a fugue on the bass part, bb. 117 ff.) and VII (a fugue on the inversion of the bass part, bb. 277 ff.). Toward the end the theme appears in a slow tempo, making a majestic effect. After the last variation there is a coda (bb. 431 ff.), in which, after a soft passage in the minor (characterized by a rapid triplet rhythm in the viola), a sudden rush of *fortissimo* E-flat major figuration in the full orchestra brings the conclusion.

Here, then, we have a large and ambitious work which manifests the affection *heroism*. The heady crescendos, coupled with sudden unexpected accentuations and exciting rhythmically driven figuration, are elements of what the French composers of the time called the *élan terrible*, which Beethoven used here to express the heroic character. In its very length it dwarfs any symphony previously composed, and the daring and magnificence of its grandiose conception have given pause to Beethoven's successors. Even late in his life when asked which of the symphonies he liked the best, Beethoven unhesitatingly named the *Sinfonia eroica*. In short, there occurred here all at once a sudden manifestation of Beethoven's power as a composer, a work that in some ways he was never to surpass.

Symphony No. 3 in E-flat Major (*Eroica*)

I

II

Marcia funebre. Adagio assai ♪=80

III

Scherzo. Allegro vivace ♩.= 116

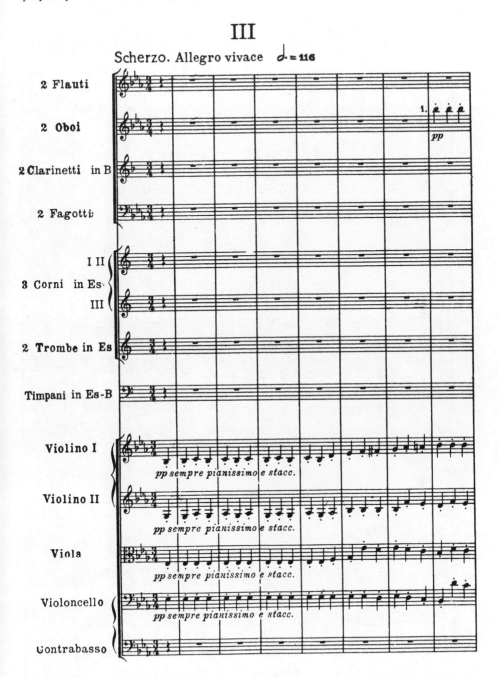

Trio

170

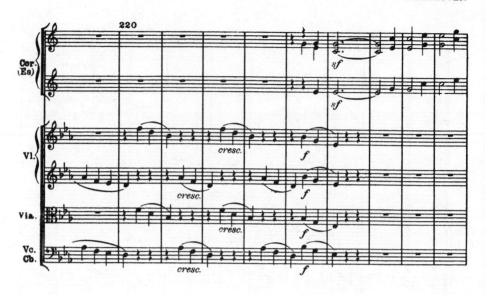

Coda

IV

Finale Allegro molto

27. String Quartet in F Major (op. 59 i)

Once the great breakthrough with respect to size and expressive range had been achieved in the Eroica Symphony, Beethoven set about doing the same thing in other genres of musical composition. This is immediately evident in the great set of three quartets of op. 59, composed in 1805–6, known as the "Razumovsky Quartets" because of their dedication to the Russian nobleman (the Czar's ambassador to Vienna) who was Beethoven's patron. The association with him is made clear by the fact that the three quartets (in F major, E minor,[1] and C major respectively) make use either implicitly or explicitly of Russian tunes. Unlike Beethoven's earlier set of quartets (op. 18) and those of Haydn and Mozart, these larger, more demanding, and brilliant pieces seem intended as much to be played before an audience as for the personal enjoyment and edification of the performers. A number of passages appear to bear this out.

This first quartet in the set is one of the most popular ever composed. It follows the four-movement scheme established for the genre, and at great length. The only departure is that the Scherzo (in B-flat major) is placed second and the slow movement (in F minor) third.

The opening movement is characterized by broadly flowing motion, interrupted every so often by disjunctive passages. The very beginning presents a good example of the progressive unfolding of the thematic material: a strong cadence to the tonic does not occur until b. 19. A secondary theme, also not clearly articulated, is at b. 60. The long development (bb. 103 ff.) features a fugal passage (bb. 184 ff.) based on the passage at b. 19 accompanied by material from the principal theme in its varied form (as at b. 30 ff.). The placement of the recapitulation is uncertain: bb. 242 or 254 are the two alternatives. A coda commences at b. 348; it has, as a quasi-orchestral culmination, a sonorous harmonization of the principal theme.

The second movement, the Scherzo, shows Beethoven's characteristic way of modifying musical forms. Usually the movement is regarded as an example of the sonata structure, though not without irregularities. The secondary

[1] For this quartet, see Godwin, *Schirmer Scores*, No. 60, pp. 895–901.

theme is at bb. 115 ff.; the development, bb. 155 ff.; the recapitulation, b. 239 ff.; and the coda, bb. 420 ff. Kerman [2] suggests that the movement be viewed instead as a scherzando with the trio appearing twice, incorporating a development section in the middle. This six-part arrangement in some ways resembles the third movements in the Fourth and Seventh symphonies, thus: scherzando in B-flat—trio in F minor (bb. 115 ff.)—development (bb. 155 ff.)—scherzando in B-flat (bb. 239 ff.)—trio in B-flat minor (bb. 353 ff.)—scherzando (bb. 420 ff.) Such a combination of traditional formal types is by no means unusual for Beethoven. Also "irregular" are the repeated notes in the principal theme, which caused much discussion when the work was new.

The very serious, song-like slow movement in F minor is less unconventional with respect to structure, since it follows the main aspects of the sonata scheme clearly enough (secondary theme, bb. 24 ff.—development, bb. 46 ff. —recapitulation, bb. 84 ff.—coda, bb. 114 ff.). The coda serves also as a link to the finale. In one of his sketch-books Beethoven referred to this movement as "the weeping willow or acacia tree over my brother's grave," which (although neither of his brothers was dead at the time) is an accurate description of its atmosphere. Particular attention should be directed to the intensely lyrical passage in the development (bb. 71 ff.).

The finale, the principal theme of which was taken by Beethoven from a Russian folk song, follows *attacca*, without a pause. This, too, is an expansive and brilliant movement in the sonata form (secondary theme, bb. 45 ff.—development, bb. 100 ff.—recapitulation, bb. 177 ff.—coda, bb. 266 ff.). The final, lingering, statement of the principal theme (bb. 310 ff.), as if reluctant to end the piece, followed by the brilliant dash to the finish, is more effective; all this is bound to impress a knowledgeable audience.

[2] Joseph Kerman, *The Beethoven Quartets* (New York, 1967), p. 106.

String Quartet in F Major

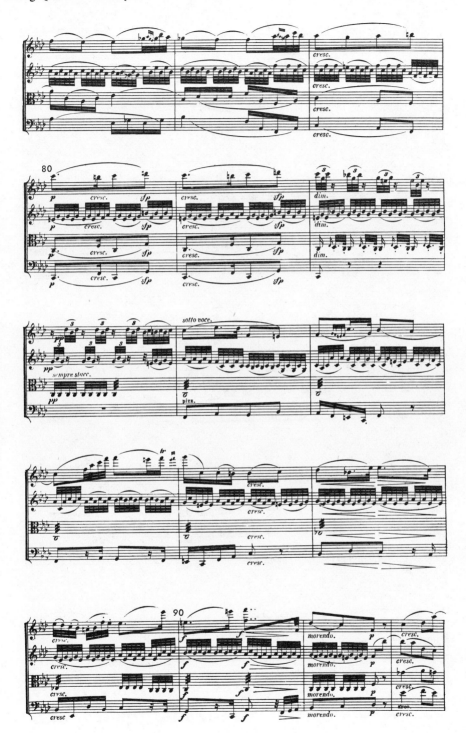

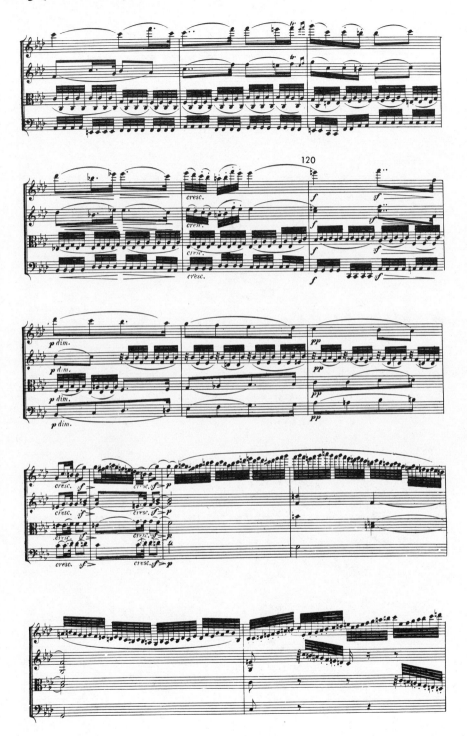

28. Trio, "Euch werde Lohn," from *Fidelio*, Act II

An important work which caused Beethoven much trouble was his single opera *Fidelio* (op. 72), or as he preferred to call it, *Leonore*. Composed between 1803 and 1805, it was not well received when given for the first time on November 20, 1805; an immediate revision, cutting the three acts down to two, given on March 29, 1806, was likewise unfavorably received. Beethoven then let the work lie for about eight years, when a thorough revision and reworking, involving the libretto as well as the music, was undertaken. This version, performed first on May 23, 1814, as last met with success, and it is in this form that the opera is performed today. There also exist four different overtures to the opera.

As already pointed out, *Fidelio* is another of those works in which Beethoven was involved with ethical—here also political—ideals. Like the *Sinfonia eroica, Fidelio* is connected with revolutionary France. The revolutionary period had been a time of political turmoil, with leaders rising and falling as different factions vied with each other to seize and hold power; people were frequently thrown into prison, and many were executed, because of their political beliefs and their opposition to the faction in power. It was a time of uncertainty, but also a time of individual heroism and of high idealism. This found artistic expression in a kind of opera popular in Paris during the 1790's, the plot of which involved a man being imprisoned for political reasons and about to be executed, who is saved at the last minute. This type of opera has been named the *rescue opera*. There are innumerable examples of rescue operas, one of the most important being Luigi Cherubini's *Les deux journées* ("The Two Days") of 1800, which was in Vienna in 1803 presented as *Der Wasserträger* ("The Water-Carrier") where it made a profound impression on Beethoven.

Fidelio is also a rescue opera. Its libretto goes back to a French opera, *Leonore*, composed by Pierre Gaveaux in 1798. The protagonist, Don Florestan (the scene is Spain), unjustly imprisoned by his rival Don Pizarro, is set free

856

by the heroic efforts of his wife Leonora. She, disguised as a boy under the name Fidelio, has won the confidence of the jailkeeper Rocco (and thus has even become engaged to Rocco's daughter Marcelline—such things are possible, even common, in opera). She succeeds in delaying the intended execution until help from outside arrives, heralded by the famous offstage trumpet signals. The idea of the heroic wife who sets her unjustly imprisoned husband free is coupled with the lofty ideas of revolutionary France: political liberty, equality, and human brotherhood. It was this combination that meant so much to Beethoven.

The excerpt presented herein, the trio in Act II, brings these very elements forcefully to expression: suffering from injustice, sympathy for the oppressed, and heroism in defiance of arbitrary authority. All this occurs in the context of an operatic ensemble of the type observed in Mozart's *Don Giovanni* (see above, p. 573). The action in this scene is simple: Florestan, in chains, gives thanks (in a broadly lyrical line) for the water given him by Leonora/Fidelio and Rocco; they, in particular Leonora, want to give him still more comfort and refreshment; Rocco at first opposes this, so that Leonora's pressure and his eventual relenting constitute the dramatic action; their renewed expressions of gratitude and sympathy bring the piece to its end.

A parallel between ensembles of this kind and the sonata structure of instrumental music has often been suggested (see the trio from *Don Giovanni* above, p. 573); it works fairly well in this case:

	Bar	
Exposition	1	*Principal theme,* A major. Florestan's gratitude.
	21	Transition. Leonora and Rocco. Quick modulation. Note "sympathy" figurative element accompanying Leonara (bb. 27 ff.).
	35	*Secondary theme,* E major. All three.
Development or Episode	49	Part I. Leonora and Rocco discuss whether or not to offer Florestan bread. New thematic material. Keys: E major going to A major and then to D major.
	69	Part II. Leonora presses her case, and Rocco finally gives in (bb. 81 ff.). Thematic material from the transition passage. Keys are unstable, modulatory, and chromatic, especially while Rocco is being convinced (bb. 75–82): D major, F minor, then enharmonically to C major.
	81	Part III. They give him the bread. Keys: C major, A minor, E major.
	92	Part IV. Re-transition. Renewed thanks from Florestan. "Sympathy" figuration

		from transition and suggestion of principal theme.
Recapitulation (Shortened)	98	*Principal theme,* A major. Varied from b. 61 by addition of Leonora and Rocco.
Coda	120	Combination of contrasting affects: Florestan—gratitude; Leonora—being overcome with remorse; Rocco—sympathy:
	120	Part I. Restated, bb. 128 ff.
	135	Part II. Varied restatement, bb. 140 ff. Shorter note-values quicken the action, producing an intensification.
	142	Part III.

Trio (*Leonora, Florestan, Rocco*), "Euch werde Lohn"

gelten.
ful-ly.

Rocco (aside to Leonora).

Ich labt' ihn gern, den ar- men Mann, es ist ja
Poor man, I'm glad I did un- bend, For, af- ter

Leonora (aside). 30

Wie hef- -tig po- chet die- ses
How wild- -ly beats this heart of

bald um ihn ge- than.
all, he's near his end.

Herz, es wogt, es wogt in Freud' und schar- - fem Schmerz.
mine, And swells, and swells as hope and fear___ com- bine.

Florestan (aside).

Be- wegt seh'
How mov'd this

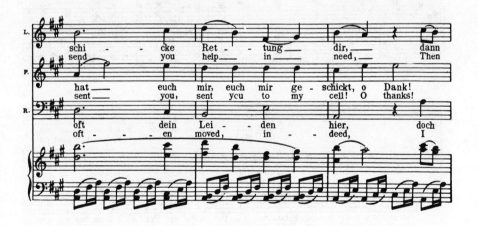

29.   Sonata No. 31 for Piano in A-flat Major (op. 110)

The late works of Beethoven have stimulated much discussion and criticism; with the exception of the Ninth Symphony they found but little understanding and acclaim among his contemporaries. Generally speaking, the large-scale form, with its emphasis on thematic development and powerful expression, gave way in his later works to music that stressed the more learned types of writing: the variation form and the fugue. The latter appeared both as an entire movement and as development within a movement in sonata form. These works also display Beethoven's continuing use of movements manifesting specific characters, such as the passionate recitative style, the *pathétique* aria style from the opera, the religious style of church music, the military march, and so on. The themes used in these late works tended to become more lyrical and melodic while losing none of their motivic character. But frequently in these works continuity is disrupted: Melodies are begun and suddenly broken off right in the middle, or, without any transition, slow, soft chords may be heard after furious figuration. The harmonic progressions are often most unusual. The overall large form, with its conception of individual movements forming the whole, was maintained by Beethoven in these works, except that it became more common for themes or passages from earlier movements to appear in subsequent ones, thus bringing in the element of cyclic form.

As an example, we may consider the Sonata for Piano in A-flat Major (op. 110) composed in 1821, which shows many of the features just mentioned. The work is in three movements. The opening one—Moderato cantabile, molto espressivo—presents an intense, lyrical theme based on a short rhythmic motive, with simple accompaniment; the secondary theme brings little contrast, and in the development the principal theme is brought to a climax. The second movement, Allegro molto—which stands for the scherzo—has a brusque chordal theme featuring irregular accentuations, along with a trio consisting mainly of figuration. From this point on, the organization of the work becomes less traditional. There follows one of those deeply felt slow movements so character-istic of Beethoven's late works, with a hint of opera in the background: a recitative and an *Arioso dolente* ("melancholy arioso"); this is followed by a fugue, after which the arioso is heard again, but with its expression heightened by the use of "sob" figures (appropriately marked *ermattet*, "exhausted"). A passage of repeated A-flat major chords in a great crescendo ushers in a repetition of the fugue, this time with the subject inverted (marked *wieder auflebend*, "coming to life again").

In many respects this composition harkens back to the fantasia-sonatas of 1801–2, particularly the one in E-flat major (op. 27 i), a type Beethoven later revived in the two sonatas for violoncello and piano (op. 102, especially the one in C major) and the Sonata for piano in A major (op. 101).

Sonata No. 31 for Piano in A-flat Major

30.   String Quartet in C-sharp Minor (op. 131)

Beethoven's last five string quartets [1] are a consummation, not only of his work with this genre of composition, but, in a way, of his work as a whole. They constitute a landmark in the history of music in Western civilization. In them we find the forms, techniques and expressive qualities of the last five piano sonatas manifested even more elaborately and comprehensively.

The famous Quartet in C-sharp minor (op. 131), composed between November 1825 and July 1826 and published the following year, departs from the four-movement scheme (as do its companions in A minor and B-flat major): It has seven movements to be played without pause, embodying different musical types, expressive characters, and techniques of composition. Beethoven jokingly referred to this in a caption he put on the copy of the score he sent to the publisher Schott in Mainz, describing the quartet as "stolen bits collected from here and there" ("*zusammengestohlen aus Verschiedenen diesem und jenem*"). Yet these elements are arranged so that one feels drawn along continuously to the climax at the end.

The succession of movements is as follows: (1) Adagio in C-sharp minor—a slow, serious, and intense fugue, what in the Baroque would have been called a ricercar, much in the tradition of the *stile antico* (i.e., resembling the polyphony of Palestrina) and thus religious in character; (2) Allegro in D major, lyrical and dance-like, almost popular in tone, in sonata form (development, bb. 48 ff.; recapitulation, bb. 88 ff.; coda, bb. 161 ff.); (3) Allegro moderato—a linking movement, very short, modulatory, ending with the cadence associated with recitative in the first violin; (4) Andante in E major—the main slow movement consisting of a theme and six variations with coda, each contrasting in character (especially prominent are the march of the second variation in bb. 65 ff.; the "liquidation," as it were, in the fifth at bb. 162 ff.; the hymn, with its densely scored accompaniment in the sixth at bb. 187 ff.; and the fantasia-like

---

[1] These quartets in order of composition are: E-flat major (op. 127), A minor (op. 132), C-sharp minor (op. 131), B-flat major (op. 130) with the Grand Fugue (op. 133)— originally the finale of the B-flat quartet, and F major (op. 125). The middle three are closely related to one another.

coda at bb. 220 ff.); (5) Presto—also in E major, a furiously dancing scherzo with a "popular" theme, the trio (*piacevole*) of which appears three times; (6) Adagio in G-sharp minor—a serious interlude, moving to (7) Allegro in C-sharp minor, the culmination, a big movement in sonata form with coda (development, bb. 78 ff.; recapitulation, bb. 160 ff.; coda, bb. 262 ff.),[2] with a violent principal theme and considerable use of counterpoint (see bb. 93 ff., 170 ff. and 313 ff.).

Karl Holz, a friend of Beethoven in these years, reported that when he raised the question concerning which of the quartets was best Beethoven responded, "Each in its own way. Art demands of us that we shall not stand still. You will find a new manner of voice treatment [part-writing] and thank God there is less lack of fantasy than ever before."[3] Yet he later acknowledged this quartet as his best.

---

[2] The use of the principal theme in its original key in the development (bb. 117 ff.) and the stress given it again in the coda (bb. 262—here in D major—and yet again in b. 349) impart a rondo-like character to the movement as well.

[3] See Alexander Wheelock Thayer, *Life of Beethoven*, edited by Elliot Forbes, II, (Princeton, 1964), p. 982.

String Quartet in C-sharp Minor

Nº4. **Andante ma non troppo e molto cantabile.**

No 6. Adagio quasi un poco andante.

Bibliography

THIS SELECTIVE LIST contains books in English that either deal in some detail with the works represented in this anthology or enunciate some of the principles and ideals that have guided the process of score selection. It is intended to serve as a point of departure for further study.

BARRET-AYRES, REGINALD. *Joseph Haydn and the String Quartet.* New York, 1974.

BEKKER, PAUL. *Beethoven.* Translated by M. M. Bozman. London and New York, 1925.

COOPER, MARTIN. *Beethoven: the Last Decade.* London, 1970.

EINSTEIN, ALFRED. *Gluck.* Translated by E. Blom. London, 1936. Reprint, New York, 1962.

————. *Mozart, His Character, His Work.* London, 1945.

GEIRINGER, KARL. *Haydn: a Creative Life in Music,* 2nd edition. New York, 1963. Reprint, Berkeley, 1968.

KERMAN, JOSEPH. *The Beethoven Quartets.* New York, 1967.

————. *Opera as Drama.* New York, 1956. Reprint, New York, 1959.

KIRKPATRICK, RALPH. *Domenico Scarlatti.* Princeton, 1953. Reprint, New York, 1968.

NEWMAN, WILLIAM S. *The Sonata in the Classic Era.* Chapel Hill, 1963. Reprint, New York, 1972.

PAULY, REINHARD. *Music in the Classic Period.* 2nd edition. Englewood Cliffs, 1973.

RATNER, LEONARD G. *Classic Music: A Handbook for Analysis.* New York, forthcoming.

RIEZLER, WALTER. *Beethoven.* London & New York, 1938. Reprint, New York, 1973.

ROBBINS LANDON, H. C. *The Symphonies of Joseph Haydn.* London, 1955. Supplement, 1961.

ROLLAND, ROMAIN. *Beethoven the Creator.* Translated by Ernest Newman. London, 1929. Reprint, New York, 1964.

ROSEN, CHARLES. *The Classical Style.* New York, 1971. Reprint, New York, 1972.